Scottish Canoe Classics

TWENTY-FIVE GREAT CANOE & KAYAK TRIPS

SECOND EDITION

Eddie Palmer

PESDA PRESS

WWW.PESDAPRESS.COM

Second edition 2015

First published in Great Britain 2007 by Pesda Press
Reprinted 2010
Tan y Coed Canol, Ceunant
Caernarfon, Gwynedd
LL55 4RN
Wales

Maps - Bute Cartographic
Printed and bound in Poland, www.lfbookservices.co.uk

Introduction

This is a book for any visitor to Scotland, not necessarily for experienced canoeists. It is a guide to the waterways, hinting at their scenery, ecology and history so that visitors (or those living in Scotland unaware of what is on their doorstep) can best enjoy this fabulous country.

The development of canoeing as a recreation and sport in Scotland started with the Victorians who became keen on sailing large canoes around the west coast of Scotland from the 1880s. There are written accounts concerning some very intrepid expeditions, long before the days of proper wet weather clothing! Whereas there are warnings in this book about exposed sections of the coastline, these fellows (and female partners) set to sea with little more than a spirit of adventure. In those days, steamers would deliver canoes and paddlers on holiday to west coast ports.

From the 1930s a select group of kayakers, in wood and canvas kayaks, set out from clubs in Edinburgh and the university cities such as Aberdeen to paddle the major rivers. Only the larger rivers and the more sheltered coastal stretches could be safely paddled in such fragile craft.

The advent of fibreglass in the early 1960s provided the first post-war boom in canoesport, followed by the explosion of rotomoulded plastic boats in the 1980s. This opened up a vast range of Scottish watercourses, including the very steepest. No longer did paddlers repair boats after every outing on water. This has led to the current boom in all types of paddlesport.

I am aware of some epic canoe voyages around Scotland's coasts, and some arduous cross-Scotland routes, but I have attempted to bring together some of the more accessible trips in this book. My personal choice was a delight to compile. It had to include the four great Scottish touring rivers of the Spey, Tay, Dee and Tweed, absolute classics, but I have also tried to choose routes from across the land.

Scotland is gaining greater interest from new canoeists who wish to explore one of Europe's last genuine wildernesses. We have a country where you can paddle and camp for days with the lochs and hills to yourself. Hopefully, the greater interest in encouraging sustainable tourism will mean more campsites and canoe trails and even more opporunities to get afloat.

Eddie Palmer

Eddie Palmer is a kayaker and canoeist with over 50 years' experience. He has sampled virtually all types of paddling, including competition in slalom and white water racing and has paddled widely outside of the UK. He is also a yacht, dinghy, and canoe sailor.

In 2004, Eddie started a journey, paddling recreational routes all over the UK and Ireland. He is now on the last 'Canoe Classic' trip in Wales. Researching Welsh Canoe Classics has taken him to many places he visited in his youth, while growing up in the West Midlands.

After 10 years on the Board of the Scottish Canoe Association (SCA), he is now both Chairman and President.

Acknowledgements

Many thanks to Mary Connacher, our 'elderly Dundee open canoe holiday group', friends and colleagues in the Scottish Canoe Association, and those paddlers I met along the way.

Special thanks to my neighbour Dave Walsh, who either took or sourced many of the photographs, and also Allan Bantick from Speyside who helped out on the wildlife information.

Photos have been acknowledged in the captions.

Using the Guide

Each route description begins with some quick reference information such as the type of water you might expect, the OS map numbers which cover the area, the places en route and the approximate distance covered by the described route. The expected shuttle time is given (the journey you may make by motor vehicle to get to the start and leave a vehicle at the finish) followed by a brief description of any expected portages (places where you may have to carry your canoe overland). It is strongly suggested that you always inspect the egress (end) of your trip before you set off, as both parking and landing places can change over time. The start and finish points for the described route are given with six figure grid references.

TYPES OF WATER

 Canals, slow-moving rivers and small inland lochs which are placid water, and easy to cope with.

Inland lochs, still with no current or tide, but which in high winds can produce large waves.

Rivers where flood conditions can make paddling difficult, and requiring a higher level of skill. The grade of any rapids is denoted from 1 to 3 within the icon.

Estuaries and sea lochs, where the direction of the tide is all-important, and usually cannot be paddled against.

Open sea, safer coastal routes suitable for placid water touring kayaks and canoes (in calm, stable weather).

The text points out the individual difficulties of the various waters. Readers with little experience are urged to look at (inspect) any water they are uncertain of, and to have access to up-to-date weather information. The mountains and lochs of Scotland are subject to frequent, sudden and local changes in weather due to the topography and prevailing weather patterns, and these should be regarded with great respect. Particular attention should be paid to weather forecasts when deciding whether to undertake one of the journeys which includes open sea.

PORTAGES

Portaging is the carrying of canoes. Portage distances have been restricted to the occasional 100m or so, around rapids, canal locks, etc. unless specifically mentioned. These portages are generally along the length of the waterway, that is downstream, not over heights.

RIVER GRADES

This book does not include whitewater paddling of grade 3 and above, except for some stretches of river where such rapids are easily portaged, or carried around. The book *Scottish Whitewater* (Pesda Press) describes these other rivers. The international river grading scale ranges from 1 to 6:

GRADE 1 Easy. Occasional small rapids or riffles, waves regular and low. Most appropriate course, with deepest water, easy to see from canoe or kayak and steer down. Obstacles e.g. pebble banks, very easy to see. Presents really no problems to paddlers able to steer canoes and kayaks. Steering is needed, especially on narrow rivers.

GRADE 2 Medium. Fairly frequent rapids, usually with regular waves, easy eddies, and small whirlpools and boils. Course generally easy to recognise, but may meander around gravel banks and trees, etc. Paddlers in kayaks may get wet, those in open canoes much less so.

GRADE 3 Difficult. Rapids numerous, and can be continuous. Course more difficult to see, landing to inspect may be wise. Drops may be high enough not to see water below, with high and irregular waves, broken water, eddies and whirlpools/boils. There is no water with rapids of above grade 3 advised in this guide. Where there are grade 3 rapids, avoiding or portaging is possible.

GRADE 4 Very Difficult. Long and extended stretches of rapids with high, irregular waves, difficult broken water, strong eddies and whirlpools. Course often difficult to recognise. High falls, inspection from bank nearly always necessary.

GRADE 5 Exceedingly Difficult. Long and unbroken stretches of whitewater with individual features, and routes, very difficult to see. Many submerged rocks, high waterfalls, falls in steps, very difficult whirlpools and very fast eddies. Previous inspection absolutely necessary, risk of injury, swims always serious.

GRADE 6 Absolute limit of difficulty. Definite risk to life.

Important Notice – Disclaimer

Canoeing and kayaking are healthy outdoor activities which always carry some degree of risk, as they involve adventurous travel, often away from habitation. Guidebooks give an idea of where to access a river, where to egress, the level of difficulty, and the nature of the hazards to be encountered. However, the physical nature of river valleys change over time, water levels vary considerably with rain, and features such as weirs, walls and landings are changed by man. Trees block rivers, and the banks erode, sometimes quickly. Coastal sections, sea lochs, and large inland lochs, are subject to the effect of tides and weather.

This guidebook is no substitute for inspection, personal risk assessment, and good judgement. The decision of whether to paddle or not, and any consequences arising from that decision, must remain with the individual paddler.

Map Symbols

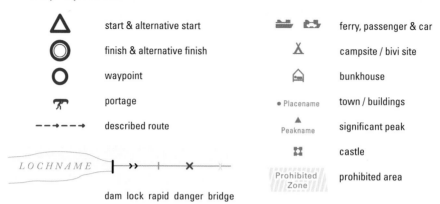

△	start & alternative start	
◎	finish & alternative finish	
○	waypoint	
🛶	portage	
– – → – – →	described route	

LOCHNAME ├──»──┤──✕──┤–

dam lock rapid danger bridge

🚢 🚢	ferry, passenger & car
⚊	campsite / bivi site
⌂	bunkhouse
● Placename	town / buildings
▲ Peakname	significant peak
♜	castle
Prohibited Zone	prohibited area

WATER LEVELS

In this guide, an indication is given of a suitable level to paddle by simple viewing on site, for example 'if the rocks are covered downstream from the bridge'. Most 'flatter rivers' can be easily seen from a road or bridge, and judgements on level are reasonably easy to make.

The SCA website www.canoescotland.org offers an invaluable service, as does SEPA (the Scottish Environmental Protection Agency) and Visit Scotland, providing current, live river levels from gauges on mostly the smaller rivers. Common sense must be used to make judgements on the levels in the larger rivers. For example, if several tributaries of the Tay are 'huge', then within a few hours, the Tay itself will also be very high.

ACCESS TO THE WATER

The Land Reform (Scotland) Act 2003 provides a clear framework for everybody to enjoy out-door sports and activities. It is important to understand the responsibilities inherent in this act, one of the best in Europe. Much of this is common sense, so ... think!

There is now a statutory right of access to most land and inland water in Scotland. The Scottish Outdoor Access Code explains how (see the page at the back of this book). As a canoeist – please pay special regard to parking near rivers or lochs, and do not park in passing places on single-track roads. Remember that parking for a van and canoe trailer requires lots of space. Whilst driving on single-track roads, allow overtaking by faster traffic (you can incur penalties for obstruction!) and pull into passing places in good time, avoiding the need to reverse trailers.

Whereas 'wild camping' can be very enjoyable, the guidance to paddlers nowadays has to be: if there is a formal campsite available, for example right next to a river or loch, you are advised to use it. The far north and west of Scotland lend themselves to real wilderness camping. Wherever you are, please be discreet, and *leave no trace!*

For more information on the Code, and contact details for river advisors, visit:

www.outdooraccess-scotland.com or www.canoescotland.com

Contents

The North-West Wilderness

An Introduction

The scenery of the north-west is amongst the most dramatic in the whole of Scotland … land and water fight each other as rocks protrude and bogs lurk amongst a tangle of large and small lochs. The area is typified by spectacular, although not high, mountains which are relatively easy to scale and very recognisable. Due to the complete lack of tree cover, these mountains appear on the horizon at every turn, and the paddler can gain access to the hinterland away from the sea with ease.

This section covers three areas: the far north of Eddrachillis Bay in Sutherland, the Coigach area north of Ullapool in Wester Ross, and the area south of the Letterewe Estate.

The far north-west of Scotland was the most notorious for the 'clearances' of the 19th century, and in Strathnaver on the north coast signs can still be seen of this ethnic cleansing. The centre of this sparsely populated area is Ullapool, a fishing village which has expanded to become a major ferry port for Stornoway, and a centre for walking and climbing. It is always lively in the summer and the Ceilidh Place Hotel frequently offers live music, and has a coffee shop and bookshop. Ullapool is well served by hotels, B&Bs and restaurants.

The road north beckons you onward all the way to the coast, with constantly awe-inspiring views around every bend in the road. Settlements are few and far between, and this is an area where the camper van comes into its own. The terrain is often so rough and boggy that wild camping is difficult.

I first experienced this area in the late 1970s on my first sea kayaking voyage in the August summer holidays. My group, from a canoe club in North East England, had spent twelve hours travelling up on what were then often single-track roads. We ended up at Kylesku, to set off the next day around to the Summer Isles (only two major headlands, we chortled).

The day dawned bright and sunny, and we departed from what was then the working ferry slipway at Kylesku, not having bothered to find a weather forecast. The day went fine as far as rounding Oldany Island, when the weather deteriorated very quickly. In mounting seas we made swiftly for the beach at Culkein … where we were storm bound in tents for the next three days, as an Atlantic depression tore across the grey landscape.

Once back on the water the trip around the Point of Stoer was, quite honestly, frightening. For most of the way one paddler did not see the others, so large was the swell. Two days later we repeated the experience around Rubha Coigach to the south – to this day I have maintained a healthy respect for this wilderness.

I'm happy to say that on returning to the area with an open canoe, greater attention was paid to the weather forecasts and we were rewarded with suitably settled conditions.

01 Kylesku Lochs & Coast

 OS Sheets 9 & 15

Ⓐ Kylesku to Loch Glencoul & Loch Glendhu | **24km**

Ⓑ Kylesku to Drumbeg | **30km**

Ⓒ Kylesku to Badcall | **31km**

Hazards	Options B and C are suitable only in calm weather.
Start	△ Kylesku ferry slipway (230 338)
Finish	◎ Kylesku ferry slipway (230 338)

Introduction

This area is a different world from Inverpolly to the south, dominated by Quinag looming on the southern horizon, with many bare rocky peaks inland. The ferry at Kylesku used to cause traffic to queue through the village, but it is much quieter today. Boat trips take tourists up the lochs to see the many seals and the UK's highest waterfall, easily accessible to the paddler. A base at Kylesku on the A894 north-south main road offers many day trips. Kylesku still has its old ferry slipways, made redundant by the bridge built in the late 1970s, and the southerly one is conveniently near to the hotel. There is no campsite here, but there are chalets and the hotel.

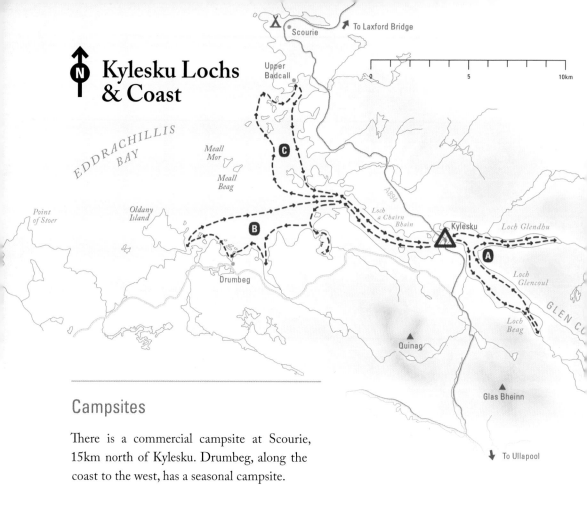

Campsites

There is a commercial campsite at Scourie, 15km north of Kylesku. Drumbeg, along the coast to the west, has a seasonal campsite.

Access & egress

For this trip there is no alternative other than to return to Kylesku.

Description

The way inland and to the south explores Loch Glencoul, and, at its head, the highest waterfall in Britain, Eas a Chual Alumn (280 278). The journey by canoe is much more pleasant than the rough and boggy 5km walk from the road, where you end up seeing the top of the fall but not the full extent of it! At the head of the loch, inside Loch Beag, there are many sheltered picnic sites. On the way up and back are islands, all with seals, and on the east side a disused hunting lodge rumoured to belong to minor royalty. Loch Glendhu adds another 12km, to its extremity and back, with a black and forbidding bare rock wall at its head.

OPTION ⓑ KYLESKU TO DRUMBEG

Access & egress

On this journey there are a number of options available. There are egress points at Loch Ardbhair (169 332); at Loch Nedd near the road and car parking (145 315); and at Loch Dhrombaig by the path up to Drumbeg village (121 331).

Description

Westward of Kylesku you will find more delights. It is about 8km (in a straight line) to the eastern side of Oldany Island. On the way there are diversions at the fjord-like Loch na Droighniche, and Loch Ardbhair. Then Loch Nedd which gives shelter amongst lush woodland, with moorings and the road conveniently nearby. The ultimate destination after that is the useful Loch Dhrombaig, and the village of Drumbeg, with a pub and car parking, making a good turning point on a round trip. Drivers have the challenge of a vehicle shuttle via the B869, one of Scotland's no-go roads for caravans, with steep hills and very tight bends. The coast after this becomes very convoluted, Culkein Drumbeg offering sheltered but shallow anchorages for larger boats. It is not advised to go further around Oldany Island. The west side of the island is very exposed to the weather and waves, which come around the corner from the Point of Stoer, one of the west of Scotland's major headlands.

Old ferry landing, Kylesku | Eddie Palmer

OPTION C KYLESKU TO BADCALL

Access & egress

In addition to a return trip to Kylesku, there is the option of finishing the journey at Bagh Chalbha bay (170 380) or Upper Badcall beach (153 415).

Description

Exploration of Eddrachillis Bay to the north reveals many interesting islands and sheltered waters, and gives a very relaxed paddle in the right weather. Loch a Chairn Bhain offers 6km of shelter followed by a further 8km heading north, winding around islands as far as the tiny beach at the hamlet of Upper Badcall.

European otter *(Lutra lutra)*

The sea lochs and rivers of the north-west of Scotland support plenty of otters. The same species is found in both fresh and salt water; there is no distinction between 'sea' or 'river' otters. This photograph was taken on the north-west coast, but prospective photographers beware, this animal can be very difficult to capture on camera unawares. Otters have a tendency to appear when least expected, bad news for those who plan an expedition to find them.

I was paddling once at the head of a group, in open canoes, on a very calm morning on Loch Caolisport in the south. I rounded a large rock into a small bay and found an otter basking on a large flat rock a few yards ahead. I was reaching for the camera when the chatter of the group behind me, oblivious to the presence of the otter, disturbed him and he swiftly disappeared.

Although major Scottish rivers such as the Tay and Spey are good habitat for otters and their favourite food of eels is plentiful, there is one aspect of river management which does not always favour them; the clearing of banks in the lower reaches for fly fishing reduces cover for bank-side creatures. The otter, secretive by nature is nervous of these open swathes and of the wooden fishing lodges. One is far more likely to glimpse an otter on a small river, where food is less abundant, as they frequently move up small ditches to forage.

Otters are beneficial to the survival of water voles, as they predate on the voles' main predator, an american interloper and relative of the otter, the mink.

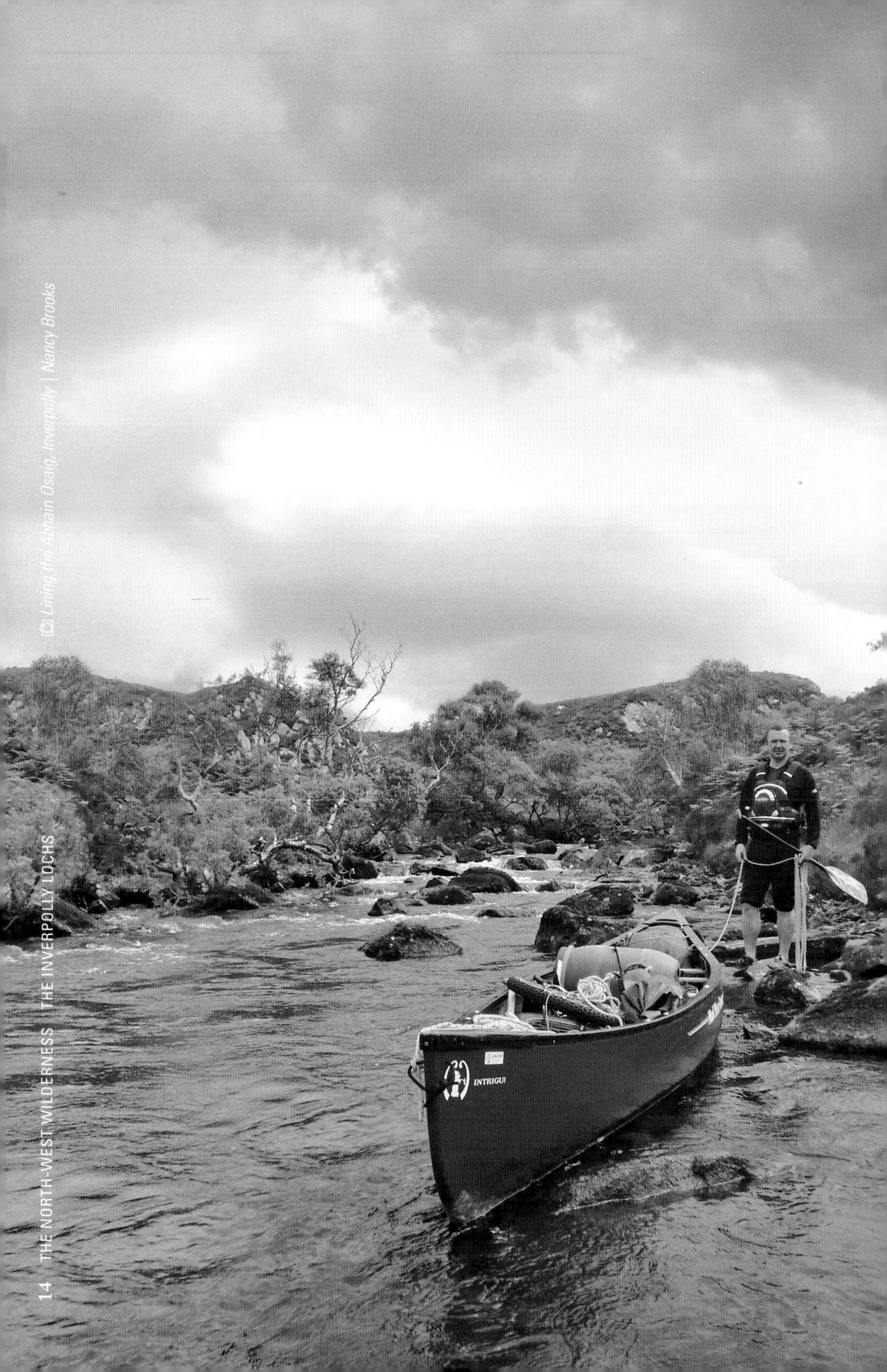

Lining the Abhain Osaig, Inverpolly | Nancy Brooks

02 The Inverpolly Lochs

 OS Sheet 15

Ⓐ Loch Sionascaig | 12km

Ⓑ Loch Veyatie & Fionn Loch | 21km

Start	△ Ⓐ Achnahaird to Lochinver road (096 156) Ⓑ Track from Elphin (214 119)
Finish	◎ Ⓐ Achnahaird to Lochinver road (096 156) Ⓑ Track from Elphin (214 119)

Introduction

Loch Sionascaig is a lovely loch in a wild setting which gives the impression of being miles from anywhere and takes the paddler into the heart of the Inverpolly Estate. It is dominated by the twin peaks of Cul Beag and Cul Mor at its eastern end, and the incredible spires of Stac Polly are always visible to the south.

Loch Veyatie and Fionn Loch is another true wilderness trip, with no real difficulties. A wonderful feature of this journey are the great views of Suilven to the north. The two separate loch trips can be joined by either of two complicated portages which are described at the end of this section.

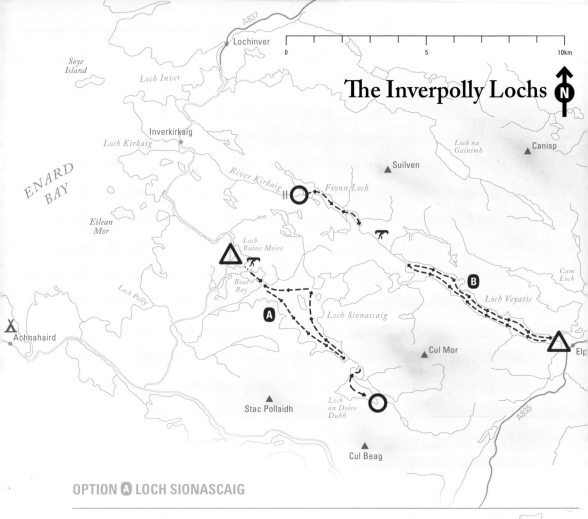

The Inverpolly Lochs

OPTION Ⓐ LOCH SIONASCAIG

Access & egress

Driving from the south, find the track to Boat Bay at (093 151). This is barely visible, as it is a bog for its first few metres. Continue onward around a tight bend until Loch Buine Moire is clearly visible on the right. On an obvious bluff above the loch there are two parking slots at a passing place. Access is down the grassy bank. Off to the left is a little bay with a boat tied up in it, and easy access to the water. Proceed across the loch to an obvious gap in the high land, and portage into Loch Sionascaig.

ACCESS TO LOCH SIONASCAIG

Campsites

The nearest formal site is at Achnahaird, a 7 mile drive away. On Loch Sionascaig there are few places to camp easily due to the rough ground. The largest island, Eilean Mor, has space at its southern tip. There is a sandy beach at the south-east end, and Loch an Doire Dhuibh, further on, also has sandy beaches.

Portages

There is a single portage of 400m from Loch Buine Moire at the start of this trip.

Description

Loch Sionascaig is 4.5km long and 3km wide, with Eilean Mor in the centre and other smaller islands dotted around the eastern side which are useful for shelter in windy weather. Expect frequent changes of weather. The portage in is fairly long and difficult (a trolley cannot be used), so make sure you go well prepared, you won't fancy nipping back for forgotten kit!

From the south-east end of Loch Sionascaig, it is possible to head upstream a short river to Loch an Doire Dhuibh. The first section is 300m long and rocky. It is necessary to line the canoes up this section. The second section is 300m of flat water which can be paddled against the flow. This brings you into the bottom end of Loch an Doire Dhuibh.

OPTION Ⓑ LOCH VEYATIE AND FIONN LOCH

Access & egress

This is another 'in and out' trip. Park in Elphin on the east side of the main road. Take care not to block the end of the track down to the loch. This track is in good condition and good for trolleys.

Escape is possible at the western end from the river outfall on Fionn Loch (123 177). The track is steep and muddy, passing down the side of the Falls of Kirkaig heading towards Inverkirkaig. After 4km it meets the coast road at a large car park where there is a coffee shop.

Campsites

The terrain is rough, so keep a good lookout for rare flat places. The nearest commercial sites to the start are at Ullapool, Achnahaird and Scourie to the north.

Description

From the track to Loch Veyatie it is worth heading over the bluff (just to the right) to see the waterfall that separates Cam Loch and Loch Veyatie. Before the track to Loch Veyatie was improved, access used to be via the small river east of Elphin, down to the Cam Loch. However, the portage around the waterfall is awkward, as it drops about 12m in four steps.

Loch Veyatie is 7km long and leads into the Uidh Fhearna, a short river that flows west into Fionn Loch (3.5km long). From here you can see the spectacular bulk of Suilven, one of Scotland's most recognisable mountains, to the north. The paddle in and back is worthwhile.

Portages

There are two possible portages that
can be used to join the two routes.

Easterly portage: After 5km of paddling up Loch
Veyatie, a bay opens out on the west (left) side. Follow
this for 1km through the narrows to the end (151 142).
A way can be found 100m up to a small lochan, out of
which flows a very small burn to the south-west. It is
1.6km down to an old house or bothy at Clais, near to
Lochan na Claise which offers a good campsite. From
here it is only a short way down north from the lochan
to a large bay on the eastern side of Loch Sionascaig.

Westerly portage: There is another reported way
across from Fionn Loch, where the river goes down to
Inverkirkaig (123 177). Head south and then south-
west 0.5km to a small loch, and then west down a burn
to Loch a Ghille. Paddle down this loch, to its exit
at the south-eastern corner, from which a burn leads
down to the north-eastern tip of Loch Sionascaig
(122 157). This route is longer than the easterly portage but easier. Both are over rough ground.

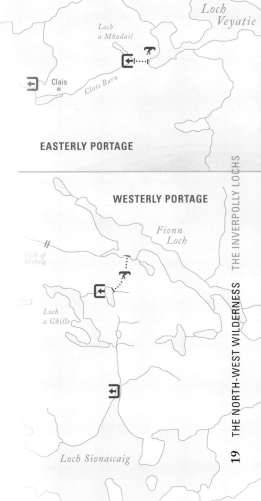

EASTERLY PORTAGE

WESTERLY PORTAGE

Portage into Loch Veyatie (Inverpolly Lochs B) | Eddie Palmer

03 Loch Maree

OS Sheet 19 | **Kinlochewe to Poolewe** | **25km**

Shuttle	Start to finish is 38km following the A832 around the southern shore.
Portages	The small rivers at the start and finish require water, without which there would be much wading.
Start	△ Kinlochewe – minor road over to Incheril (034 619), or in low water on the side of Loch Maree at a parking spot (001 650).
Finish	○ Poolewe Bridge (858 808), or in low water on a B road past Tollie Farm to Tollie Bay (869 781).

Introduction

The loch is beautiful, with the peak of Slioch visible above the loch to the north and the Torridon mountains to the south, Beinn Eighe being the most obvious at the head of the loch. The loch is one of the largest in this part of Scotland, being 20km long and giving good views all along its length. Where the islands are situated the loch is 3.5km wide, large enough to give an impression of wilderness, even though the main road follows the south bank for much of its way. Paddling on Loch Maree has been contentious in the past. The situation has now been smoothed over by the new Scottish Outdoor Access Code.

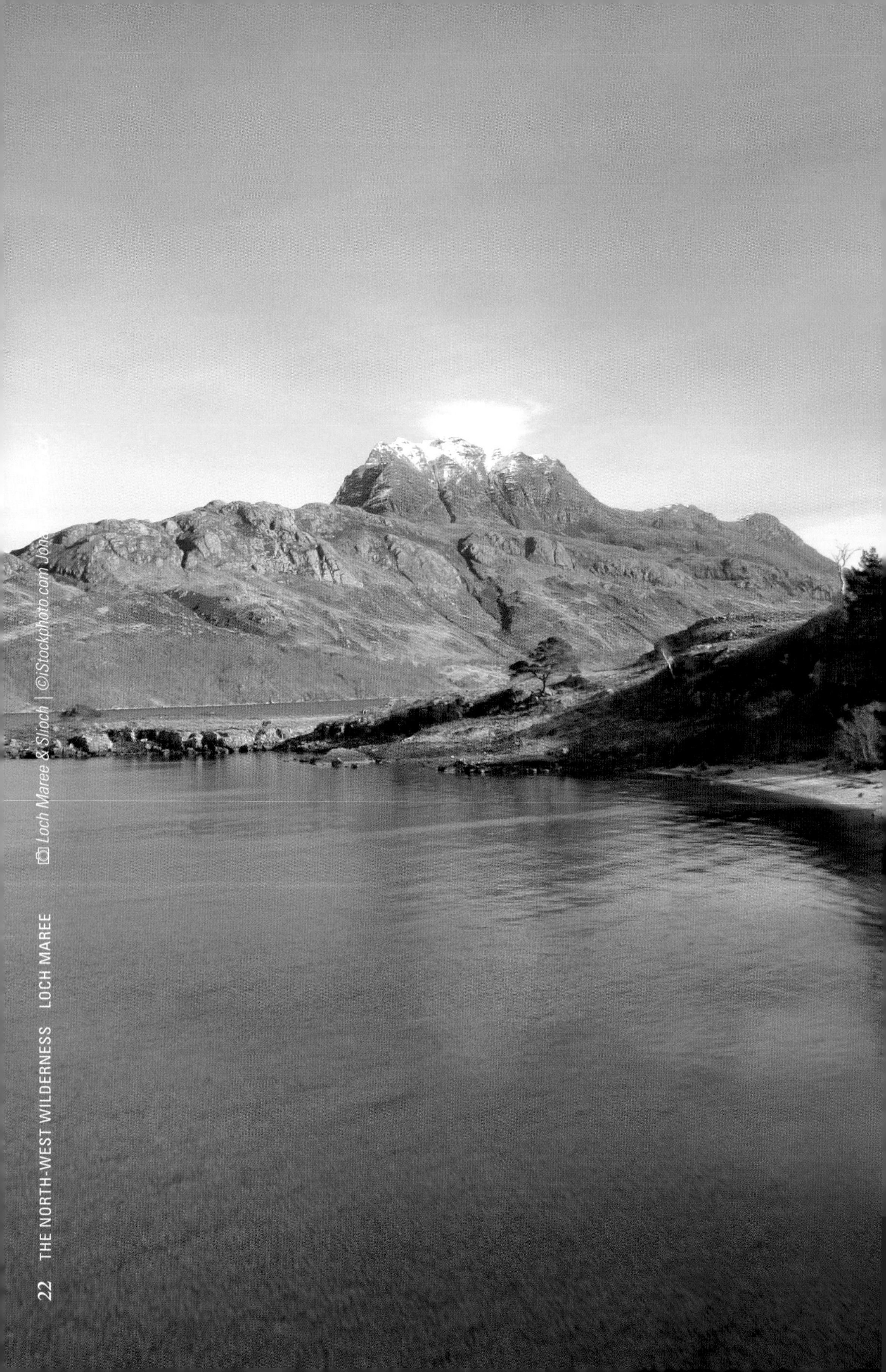

Loch Maree & Slioch | ©iStockphoto.com Jona

Access & egress

The loch is within the Beinn Eighe and Loch Maree Islands National Nature Reserve (designated 2014) managed by Scottish National Heritage. It is important that before paddling you go to the visitor centre at the south-east corner of the loch to ask for advice. The islands you will paddle around have several international conservation designations and in spring, birds nesting on the islands are fully protected.

The centre is at NH 018 630, IV22 2PA. There is ample parking, toilets, and exhibits. The nearest access to water from here is a car park at NH 001 650, IV22 2PD.

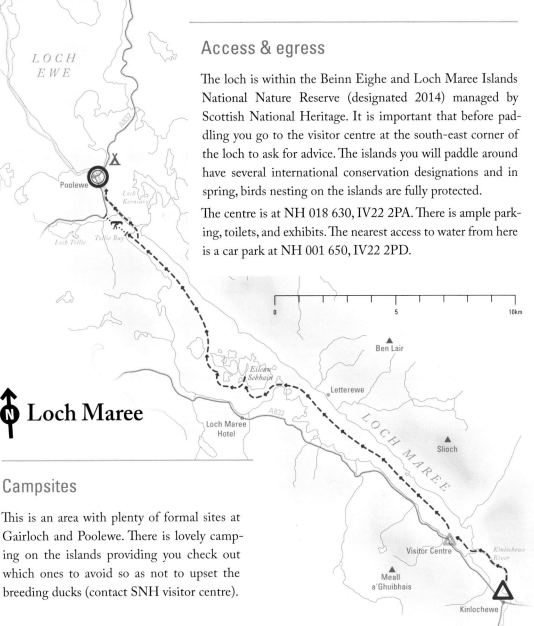

Loch Maree

Campsites

This is an area with plenty of formal sites at Gairloch and Poolewe. There is lovely camping on the islands providing you check out which ones to avoid so as not to upset the breeding ducks (contact SNH visitor centre).

Description

The loch is yet another Scottish gem, with six or seven large islands, and many more smaller ones in the centre, Eilean Sebhain being the largest. Unlike lochs to the north, Loch Maree has wooded slopes and is relatively sheltered from the worst of the weather coming in from the west. Letterewe Estate with its fishing and landing piers lies about 9km down the loch. The northern shore is wild, with a backdrop of some of the most famous mountains in Scotland, an area to pass through slowly and to savour.

© Loch Maree viewed from Kinlochewe end | Eddie Palmer

Loch Maree has gone down in access history as being something of a flashpoint. The situation became gradually worse during the 1980s and early 90s, with a threatened mass paddle, after incidents of intimidation. It was alleged that the issue was the black-throated divers that breed on the islands, and should of course be protected. Suspicions remain that the dispute was more to do with fishing from boats with small outboards and a dislike of canoeists. The situation has settled down but paddlers should seek information in advance on how to avoid disturbing the wildlife (contact SNH visitor centre).

I once paddled from the northern end of the loch down the River Ewe, where a fisher-person screamed at me that the river was not navigable. Well, our boats floated fine down it!

Loch Maree inspires exploration. When I realised that the Kinlochewe River was paddleable and that the deeper tributary, the A'Ghairibhe, could be done by kayak from higher up, I had the idea that Glen Docharty, which goes east over the watershed to Achnasheen and the eastern rivers, could be a portage route for a west to east coast trip, to include Loch Maree. Soon after I was a bit put out when two friends of mine paddling from Achnasheen to Conon Bridge found graffiti in a bothy suggesting another group had completed that very trip! Eventually I paddled it myself.

Wild animals in Scotland

One of the large estates in the north of Scotland, in east Sutherland, recently asked for planning permission to enclose a large area where reintroduced animals such as wolves, bears and lynxes could be released. The idea is controversial and permission was denied.

What is certainly true is that the unchecked expansion of the red deer population will, and already is severely damaging trees, and the reintroduction of predator species could help to balance the ecology.

European beavers are now very common in the Tay system, their signs e.g. chewed trees and branches can be seen in many places. At the time of preparing the second edition (April 2015) the Scottish Government is about to announce whether two colonies of beavers, one in Knapdale, Kintyre, the other in Tayside, will be allowed to remain.

Perhaps the most secretive and rarely seen animal, the wild cat, illustrates the dangers of leaving wild animals to fend for themselves, as the population is only slowly recovering from years of killing by gamekeepers. I have only seen a wild cat twice in eleven years of living in Scotland, both when crossing roads in the Angus glens at dusk.

The Great Glen

An Introduction

The great divide across Scotland yields many paddling possibilities. The Caledonian Canal uses three lochs to cross the country as well as flights of locks on short stretches of canal. Rivers abound, both whitewater and flat.

The whole glen is a paradise for walkers and cyclists as well as canoeists, offering the mildest and easiest cross-country route across Scotland. It is still an epic trip, with a great sense of satisfaction for those who complete it. The route has two great advantages: it is nearly at sea level, avoiding the worst of the Scottish weather, and it is a straight line, from south-west to north-east, making navigation simple. As the prevailing wind is usually from the west, it is preferable to travel west to east.

Many types of boat have been used for this trip, the current favourite probably being sea kayaks. A choice which becomes obvious when strong winds blow on the expanse of Loch Ness. However, open canoes and touring kayaks are also very suitable.

The city of Inverness is the rapidly expanding capital of the north of Scotland. Not long ago it was the fastest expanding city in Europe. Inverness is useful for shopping, and has backpacker accommodation as well as the usual hotels and B&Bs.

Several interesting glens come down to Inverness from the west and south. Two of these contribute to the Great Glen route itself: the quiet and rarely visited Strathglass, and the whole of the Glen Garry water route, which joins at Invergarry.

The area offers much to the visitor. To name just a few, there is Fort William, the self-styled 'outdoor capital' of Scotland, the industrial heritage of the Caledonian Canal, the quiet glens and mountains, and the city of Inverness.

Urquhart Castle, Loch Ness | Dave Walsh

© *River Beauly, Eileanaigas | Dave Walsh*

© Eileanaigas Gorge | Eddie Palmer

04 Rivers Glass & Beauly

⊡ **OS Sheet 26** | **Cannich to Aigas** | **23km**

Shuttle	20 minutes for the 16 miles up the A831.
Start	△ Cannich bridge (346 314).
Finish	⊙ Aigas Dam (474 436).

Introduction

The Glass and Beauly are little-known rivers, the latter conceals the great secret of the Aigas Gorge, an unusual feature on a flat river, and a consequence of the dam. The Beauly is barely visible when driving up the valley, whereas the Glass is exposed with grassland down to its banks.

This paddle is an often overlooked gem; from the Affric foothills, through lofty cliff amphitheatres, mixed woodland, forest and flat grassland. This is Chisholm country, with the Clan seat at Cromar near the start of the paddle, and their current base at Erchless Castle lower down near Struy. An annual clan gathering occurs at Cannich and Erchless each July. Wildlife abounds, eagles and ospreys above, otters, mink and pine martens on the banks and in the woods. Otters are seen in the Aigas Gorge quite often at daybreak.

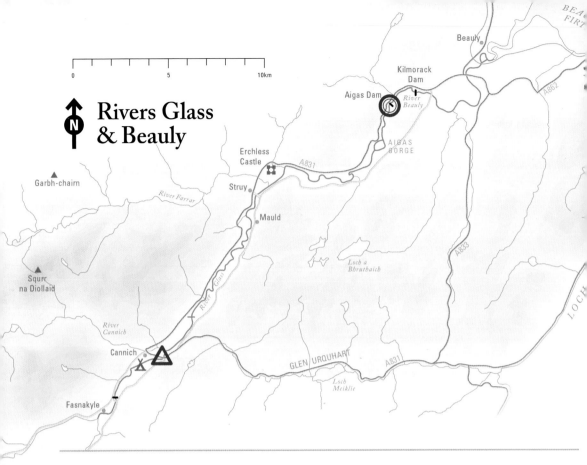

Water level

There are frequent, almost daily releases from the Fasnakyle Dam upstream from Cannich, giving a rise of 20-30cm. Looking downstream from Cannich bridge, the gravel rapids should be nearly covered; if they are well covered, the river is high and fast. When approaching Aigas Island, the river becomes a reservoir.

Access & egress

From the A831 there are several places on the Glass where it meets the road; at Struy bridge, where the Glass becomes the Beauly, upstream on the Farrar (403 395); after this, access is difficult, and a two day trip could usefully be broken at Struy. A day trip could be undertaken in 6-7 hours, maybe more if there is no release.

Campsites & accommodation

The river divides neatly into two days: Cannich to Mauld (Struy bridge), a distance of 12km and Mauld to Aigas, a distance of 14km. There is a campsite and Youth Hostel at Cannich. Both Cannich and Tomich have B&Bs, and good meals can be had at the Tomich Hotel, Slaters Arms, Cannich, and the Cnoc and Glass restaurants in Struy.

Description

The river is grade 1, possibly reaching grade 2 on some corners in high water. Occasionally fallen trees may create a hazard. It is popular with open canoeists as it inspires a feeling of trepidation, yet is not remote at all.

From Cannich village there are two access points; from the centre, drive one mile down the road to the bridge, and from the campsite, half a mile downstream on the left bank. The river meanders across a flat plain, and runs fast when there is a dam release. Shingle banks alternate with deeply wooded sections near the road. Halfway down to Struy is a section with islands and channels.

After Mauld bridge (access is upstream on the left bank) the swift waters of the River Farrar join from the left. There are more long bends with some sharp corners. A long straight section leads to the wooded Aigas Island which was the historical seat of the Lovats. The original family home was demolished by a Canadian millionaire, and a massive new castle was completed in 2009.

The island can be circumnavigated, but better still is to paddle down the left-hand branch of the reservoir behind the Aigas Dam. Rock walls rise steeply, unusual for a flat piece of water. Turn right at the end of the island to see the bridge over to the island and the new house.

Paddle another couple of kilometres between high rock cliffs to get to the dam. Ospreys often fish these waters, a fantastic sight for those lucky enough to see them.

The carry-out to the road is a bit strenuous. The path is about 100m before the dam on the left bank. It rises diagonally right between the trees before turning left and joining the steep road down to the dam. There is usually enough parking by the road.

Osprey *(Pandion haliaetus)*

Ospreys are one of the great wildlife success stories for Scotland. These great birds were first reintroduced in the 1960s to Loch Garten, near Aviemore and now they can be seen outside of the three main RSPB reserves that feature viewing facilities.

Ospreys now breed on Bassenthwaite Lake in Cumbria, at Rutland Water in eastern England, and in the Glaslyn valley, North Wales. The Scottish birds favour Scots pine forests, fresh water lochs and rivers such as the quiet Beauly.

The birds have a wingspan of around two metres, and with their pale underparts and serrated wing-tips they are unmistakeable. They winter mainly in West Africa, marked Scottish birds being seen frequently in Gambia by tourists watching the same birds in summer back home.

Ospreys are astute when it comes to choosing nesting sites, they use dead trees but also the tops of electricity poles and pylons. Their one necessity is to be in the vicinity of fresh water with a supply of fish. Their presence denotes unpolluted water.

📷 *Young osprey | Allan Bantick*

The vastness of Loch Ness | Eddie Palmer

05 Great Glen Canoe Trail

 OS Sheets 41, 34 & 26 | Banavie to Dochgarroch | 83km

Shuttle	60 miles each way up the east side of Loch Lochy, and then west side of Loch Oich and Loch Ness on the A82, about 1 hour 40 minutes. Slow and dangerous road in summer.
Portages	Canoes are not allowed in the locks of the Caledonian Canal. The longest flights are at Neptune's Staircase at Corpach, and at Fort Augustus.
Start	△ Banavie on B8004 (115 772).
Finish	◯ Dochgarroch Lock (618 404).

Introduction

This route is part of the Great Glen Canoe Trail, the first planned canoe trail in Scotland, which opened officially in 2012. Together with the Great Glen Walking and Cycle Trails, the canoe trail is operated by Scottish Canals. The website www.greatglencanoetrail.info contains a surfeit of useful information. Online registration for the trail (for safety reasons) gives access to maps, outdoor and access information, safety guidance (there is now an RNLI inshore rescue boat on Loch Ness), camping advice, etc.

On the ground, the trail includes low-level pontoons for canoes, additional campsites and access to toilets and showers. The trail was put together by a partnership that includes the SCA. The 'merchandise' part of the website sells the official guidebook (also produced by Pesda Press).

The nature of the three lochs encountered is different, Loch Lochy is of medium size, dark with much forestry to the west, Loch Oich pretty and wooded, and Loch Ness, well … just very large, and sometimes intimidating.

Caledonian Canal

The Caledonian Canal makes this cross-country trip possible, and provides ready made holidays for many people. Kayakers and canoeists are warned to watch out for the people handling cruisers on the canal. Most of them are first-timers, and I've heard that many choose a holiday in this area "because there's more room than on the Norfolk Broads". This translates as 'when not under control on the lochs, there is more room in which to gather speed before hitting something'.

The canal is indeed an engineering marvel, passing through beautiful scenery all the way. The work on the canal commenced in 1803, using plans drawn by Thomas Telford, following the surveying in the 1770s by another famous son of Scotland, James Watt. It was one of the building schemes initiated by the government (an early 'welfare-to-work' scheme) to try and stem the enormous emigration from the Highlands, which threatened total depopulation.

It was obviously, even by today's standards, a huge project and the timescale and costs were soon outstripped (sounds familiar?). By the time it opened seventeen years later in 1822, the budget of £840,000 was more than double the original.

Unfortunately, the greatest depth had been shaved to only 14ft, too shallow for many of the larger ships, so the canal was not a success initially. More work between 1844 and 1847 increased the depth, but by then many of the sailing ships had been replaced by steam vessels which could make the journey around the top of Scotland much more easily in the winter.

The route of the Caledonian Canal stretches 22 miles through man-made canal, and 38 miles along three lochs. There are twenty-nine locks. The best places to view boats are Neptune's Staircase near Corpach and Banavie at the southern end, Fort Augustus, and Muirtown basin at Inverness.

For the river paddler who tackles the River Lochy, it is possible to see the original course of the river out of Loch Lochy where the Spean joins the Lochy at Muconomir power station. The river was first diverted for the canal, and then the hydro station was built later.

There are many interesting websites about the canal. The site provided by Keith and Lois Forbes (www.treasuresofbritain.org) gives detailed information on the canal, boats, hotels and travel links.

Water level

The level of the River Oich can be judged at Bridge of Oich, an old footbridge, by looking up at the weir where the river leaves the loch.

Campsites

There are campsites in the Fort William area, along Loch Ness and at Dochgarroch. There is a site at Lewiston near Drumnadrochit, but it is some distance from the water. The availability of wild campsites is dwindling, but there are wooded areas near Invergarry and in Urquhart Bay.

The Canoe Trail has its own sites on Loch Lochy, on Loch Oich, and two on the 'south side' of Loch Ness.

See www.greatglencanoetrail.info

Great Glen Canoe Trail

Access & egress

There are may places at which to break your journey. The following points are suggested:

- Gairlochy (176 841) with limited parking
- Bunarkaig (186 877)
- Laggan Locks (287 963)
- Great Glen Water Park (301 983)
- Parking and picnic site on Loch Oich (303 989)
- Bridge of Oich (337 036)
- Fort Augustus at the foot of the locks (380 093)
- Rubha Ban campsite (425 150)
- Alltsigh Youth Hostel (458 190)
- Inverfarigaig (521 239)
- Dochgarroch lock, marina and campsite (618 404).

Description

The locks have to be portaged and so this journey starts just along from Banavie, with 10km to Gairlochy and Loch Lochy. Gairlochy has no parking, a real problem.

The journey passes quickly into pleasant green rural scenery, with the aqueduct over the River Loy a bit more than halfway along. Whitewater paddlers frequently run the Loy including the tunnel in the winter.

Loch Lochy is some 15km long and ends in Laggan Locks. The loch opens out to the west at first where the River Arkaig debouches into the loch at Bunarkaig. A forest lines the west bank, and the road runs along the east side. At Laggan Locks there is a landing platform on the north side behind Ivy Cottage. Portage along the north towpath for 250m and access via a low level pontoon at the far end.

Laggan to the swing bridge at the entrance to Loch Oich is a mere 2.5km, here the scenery becomes more wooded and appears busier (due to the lesser expanse of Loch Oich). The navigation for ships is buoyed, but the canoeist can follow more interesting little passages. Loch Oich is 6km long, dominated mid-way by the Glengarry Castle Hotel on the western bank. The Garry can just be made out as it joins the loch through thick woods.

A choice now has to be made; whether to stay on the canal or paddle the River Oich. The river is a super introduction to moving water for the open canoeist. The Glen Garry hydro system fills Loch Oich, and this tops up the Caledonian Canal to the north (on its way down to Inverness) and raises the River Oich. There is a release down the Garry every Tuesday, so the overflow

reaches the Oich mid-morning. Don't have a break halfway down and leave canoes untethered as the river may rise very quickly by around 30cm.

Land at the piece of ground that has a parking area between the river and canal, as entry onto the Oich is at the historic Bridge of Oich, now a footbridge. The river leaves over an obvious weir on the left side. If the weir is flowing well, with an obvious way down the left side, the Oich is full. It can be paddled in low water but will require some wading.

Easy shingle rapids between wooded banks and meadows lead the paddler pleasantly down to a halfway point, where a dry overflow weir marks the canal on the right bank, and Kytra Lock just along the towpath. This is a good stopping point as a trickier rapid lies just around the corner, and guaranteed amusement can be had at the canal locks as less experienced sailors negotiate the locks.

The next left-hand bend leads into a sharp right-hander, with a greater gradient. There are easy routes down but plenty of rocks.

The river has regular small rapids after this, finishing with a bit of a surprise about 1km from Fort Augustus. There is a definite drop, with a careful choice of route required. The town arrives suddenly. The main road bridge is followed by an old footbridge, and the river flows down to Loch Ness, with a turn to the right into the end of the canal. A stop can be made by getting out onto one of the many boat pontoons, taking care not to block access for other users. The road alongside is useful for parking vehicles for a short time.

If following the canal, it is 8km to the Fort Augustus locks, with Kytra Lock halfway along (all canal locks need to be portaged).

Fort Augustus is always busy in the summer, the locks in the middle of the town are surrounded by cafés and pubs, great for boat watching.

After Fort Augustus, Loch Ness stretches to the horizon and is to be treated with respect. When a wind blows, the fetch can create quite large waves, and paddling against it is nearly impossible.

Just after Fort Augustus on the right is the major civil engineering project of the Glen Doe hydro scheme, the largest in the UK since the 1950s. You will see the exit tunnel from the underground power station, with the water to power it being taken from the headwaters of the Doe, Tarff and others (the reservoir covering a large area in the Monadhliath Mountains to the east).

Loch Ness is unremittingly steep-sided. The main road follows the western bank, with a campsite halfway up. Stopping and camping places can be found on the eastern shore (called 'South Side'), and the Canoe Trail has developed two new sites along here. There is a B road following the east bank from Foyers up to the end, which is much quieter. The loch is 38km long, and the most obvious feature is the inlet at Urquhart Castle and Drumnadrochit some 28km up. This area becomes very busy with tourists in summer but has many amenities.

After a further 10km Loch Ness narrows, and gives way to Loch Dochfour. This ends after 2km with the canal leaving on the left, and the River Ness on the right. The final point on the canal route is at the lock about 400m along.

If taking the Ness, there are islands, with the route down the right side, two broken weirs taken on the left side of the river, a rapid on the right side, and then Holm Mills weir, taken by a chute which is obvious, about halfway along the long left wall. It is about 6km down to Inverness, with a useful egress at the Ness islands on the left side at a white metal footbridge, with parking.

 Upper Loch Garry from north bank | Eddie Palmer

06 Glen Garry

OS Sheets 33 & 34 | Loch Quoich, Upper River Garry, Loch Poulary & Loch Garry | 46km

Shuttle 25 miles, taking one hour, one way.

Start △ Bridge on north side of Loch Quoich (016 040).

Finish ○ Loch Garry dam (277 023).

Introduction

This area is a true wilderness with lovely unspoilt rivers and lochs. The route is easy to complete, with escape possible at any time using the road to the north. It can give a good three days' paddling. Many climbers and walkers use Loch Quoich to gain access to the Munros to the south and west. Take care on the narrow, single-track road up the glen, and do not block passing places by parking or stopping to view the river.

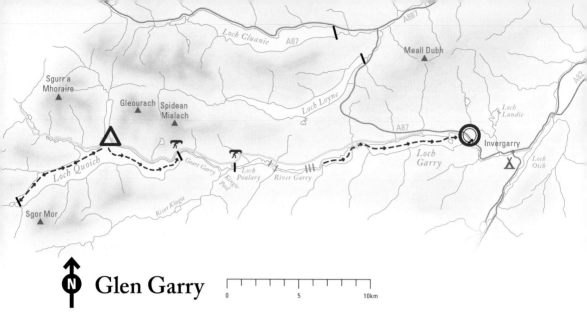

Glen Garry

0   5   10km

Water level

The only downside to this route is that the Loch Poulary/River Garry system is fed more by the River Kingie than the Geart Garry (down from the dam), so the 3km of the Geart Garry can be a scrape. Below Kingie Pool, the place where the rivers join, there is nearly always water. Travel up the glen to view the Geart Garry above the Glen Garry dam.

Access & egress

Access is via the A87 to Skye, turning off on the B road (single track) to Kinloch Hourn along the side of Loch Garry. It is then a drive of about 20 miles, taking an hour, to reach the point where the road starts to leave Loch Quoich (989 036). If Loch Quoich is low, access wherever the road is near water.

The following other access and egress points are suggested:

- Loch Quoich dam (070 025)
- The entrance to Glen Garry dam (103 013) although the gate across the road is often locked
- The Kinloch Hourn road to Loch Poulary (126 017)
- The road onto Upper Loch Garry, at the fish farm (190 022)
- The road onto Loch Garry at the slipway (210 022).

Campsites

There are two formal sites in Invergarry. Elsewhere, wilderness camping is the only option. The site at the western end of the loch, surrounded by high mountains, is unforgettable.

Description

Loch Quoich is a bare, sometimes gloomy place, hemmed in by mountains. When the loch has dropped several metres the sides are rock and mud but the scenery makes a sometimes awkward launching worthwhile. From the bridge over the northern arm of the reservoir it is a paddle of 9km west to a small dam. The reservoir was formed by damming gaps to both the west (a minor gap) and the east, a much larger one.

To the south-west, through the gap of the pass, is the conical shape of Sgurr na Ciche. The campsite at the dam is ringed by nine Munros (mountains of over 3,000 feet). From this dam it is a hard 10km walk south-west up the glen of the Allt Coire Nan Gail and Allt Bealach na h-Eangair to a *bealach* (pass) east of Sgurr nan Ciche, and then down the Allt Coire na Ciche to Loch Nevis. Paddlers do sometimes portage along this route, which rises to a height of 400m. There is also a route north-west all the way through to Barrisdale Bay, another hard slog as is everything in Knoydart. This goes up an obvious track to Lochan nam Breac, and then climbs high above it on the north side, round the head of the upper waters of the River Carnach for 4km, and joins a main path up Luinne Bheinn, one of the three gems of Knoydart. The route descends 3km to Glen Barrisdale, and a further 2km on the flat to the beach. Great country for wild walking.

From the head of Loch Quoich east to the dam is 14km, with a carry over the dam via the road. The Geart Garry is a 3km small, rocky river with occasional rapids. The road comes near about

halfway down to a junction with the river Kingie at Kingie Pool. From here on, the river is far bigger. After 1km the Glengarry dam is portaged on the left side. This is a possible escape route. The following 3km long Loch Poulary provides a rest before the River Garry. The road down the glen is high up on the north bank, amongst bracken in summer. The right bank is conifer woodland.

The loch becomes the river at two islands, Eilean a Mhorair, and the broad and fast flowing river reminds me of rivers in northern Sweden or Finland. There is an almost continuous rapid, commencing at the islands and flowing under an estate bridge, and there are many channels down a rocky bed with powerful water. There are no appreciable drops but it is a committing stretch in an open canoe. The views are mainly blocked by dense conifer forest.

The River Garry remains broad and fast until a plethora of islands 2km downstream. There are pleasant campsites amongst grass and pines on some of the islands, usually free from midges in summer. There is a real wilderness feel, and campers are out of the way of estate activities. The only habitation for miles around is the Tomdoun Hotel high up on the left bank, 1km downstream of the islands.

Loch Garry is 11km long, passing under an estate bridge at the narrows a third of the way down. At the narrows, looking up to the high ground on the left you will see the A87, and a viewing point where many of the famous photographs of Glen Garry are taken from.

Egress at the end of the loch is onto a track on the left side, just before the dam. There are several other rough surface lay-bys used by anglers. Below the dam is the whitewater River Garry, very busy whenever there is a release. It is 5km down to Invergarry, a small village with a shop and hotel.

ALTERNATIVE ITINERARIES

It is worth paddling on Loch Quoich with a night's camp at the western end. If a portage is undesirable it is also worth paddling up Loch Garry for the scenery.

The North East twixt Dee & Spey

An Introduction

The north-east of Scotland is a treat for the historian and those keen on castles. For the canoeist, it is bounded by two of the largest rivers in Scotland, the Spey and the Aberdeen Dee. A well-marked road trail connects twelve castles across the north of Aberdeenshire, dating from the 16th and 17th centuries. Another eight properties of interest are situated just off the trail.

The trail starts on Royal Deeside just outside Aberdeen, and finishes at Banff on the spectacular north coast, along from Fochabers and Spey Bay.

Drum Castle lies just west of Peterculter, off the A93, north of the Dee. It is the embodiment of vernacular architecture, having been redeveloped over 650 years by twenty-one generations of the Irving family. There is a medieval tower, a Jacobean mansion house, and more modern additions made by the Victorians.

A little way up the main road heading upriver is Crathes Castle, situated on an estate granted to the Burnett family by Robert the Bruce in 1323. The tower house is 16th century. There is plenty to see in the house and the gardens are magnificent, especially in May and June. Great yew hedges separate eight gardens and date from 1702. The large grounds include farmland, woodland and freshwater habitats. There is also a shop and café.

The road trails away from the Dee, north-west up the A980. Craigievar Castle has stood in woodland to the west of the road for the last four centuries. William Forbes built the Great Tower in the 17th century, and his family lived here until the National Trust for Scotland took over the castle in 1963.

Continuing up the Dee valley, there are also castles at Balmoral (the Queen's Scottish residence every August), and Braemar.

Onward from Craigievar, the trail joins the A944 and heads west for Kildrummy on the north bank of the River Don. Here there is a ruin of a 13th century castle dismantled after the first Jacobite rising in 1715 (though the layout is still apparent). This was the stronghold of the Earls of Mar. Nearby are attractive gardens, with a burn spanned by a replica of the Brig of Balgownie in Aberdeen.

The road winds up the attractive upper valley of the Don. Corgaff Castle is at the bottom of the hill leading up to the notorious Cockbridge to Tomintoul road, often blocked by snow in winter. The restored castle is in a spectacular position, surrounded by open moorland. Dating from 1537, it played a major role in the Jacobite risings of 1715 and 1745, and was converted into barracks for Hanoverian troops in 1748.

Our route now turns back east, past Kildrummy and Alford, to Castle Fraser near Kemnay, south of the B993 road. The Frasers built this imposing building between 1575 and 1636. As well as the large house there are gardens and a safe, yet imaginative, children's play area.

We head north next through Kintore, Inverurie (the largest town in this part of the county) and then Oldmeldrum.

In the ancient area of Formantine, east of Oldmeldrum is the ruin of Tolquhon Castle, the tower of which was built in the early 15th century and expanded in the late 19th century under the ownership of William Forbes.

North from Pitmedden through Tarves is Haddo House and its extensive gardens. These are more modern than many on the trail, being designed by William Adam in 1732 and refurbished in 1880.

The trail then heads west back to the A947, then north to Fyvie Castle at the village of Fyvie on the main road. This is a magnificent 800 year old castle, with towers associated with each of the five successive occupying families: the Prestons, Meldrums, Setons, Gordons and Forbes-Leith. There is a rich portrait collection here.

A few miles further on at Turriff is Delgatie Castle. Mary Queen of Scots stayed here in 1562 after the Battle of Cirrichie. The building is still lived in, though the oldest standing parts do not pre-date 1570.

A scenic drive can be taken across country through the isolated valley of the Deveron, west towards Huntley. The river offers excellent views of the castle, from a 12th century motte and bailey to a medieval tower house and defence earthworks dating from the Civil War.

The trip finishes with a drive up the A97 to Duff House at Banff, built by William Adam between 1735 and 1740. It is a classic Regency house, with fine art and furniture collections.

The coast east from Spey Bay used to be one of Scotland's best-kept secrets; it has become more popular recently, partly due to the fame of the village of Pennan in the film 'Local Hero'. The area has many unspoilt fishing villages, deserted sandy beaches, majestic cliffs and a quiet farming hinterland. As yet it is untouched by tourism.

Above Knockando, River Spey | Nancy Brooks

07 River Spey

OS Sheets 35, 36 & 28 | Loch Insh to Spey Bay | 96km

Shuttle	55 miles, 2 hours, via A9, A95 Aviemore to Grantown and Rothes, B9015 to Fochabers, and B1094 to Spey Bay.
Start	△ Loch Insh Watersports Centre (838 045) – ask permission to launch; parking is free, but there is a launching fee.
Finish	◯ Spey Bay (349 656).

Introduction

The Spey is a classic Scottish touring river. The 1930s saw the first parties travelling up from England to take a three or four day journey down a picturesque strath amongst some of Scotland's most famous whisky distilleries. It is a fast river, unusually fastest in its lower reaches toward the sea, with a variety of scenery and interesting rapids that are not too stressful for the inexperienced paddler.

In dry summers there might be some wading down small shingle rapids, but most seasons provide fast and adequate water.

The river has a reputation for being fished by friendly anglers. Much effort goes into maintaining good relationships between recreational paddlers, commercial canoeing and rafting interests, anglers and landowners.

The Spey flows through Aviemore, a major skiing and tourism centre with plenty of facilities. Further south, just off the A9 is the Highland Wildlife Park, with native animals including the largest pack of wolves in Britain. The middle of the valley is in the heart of the 'Whisky Trail' with famous distilleries at Knockando, Carron, Daluaine, Aberlour and Rothes, and with more off the direct route at Dufftown and Keith. At Spey Bay, the end of the river introduces the different scenery and interests of the north-east coast and its fishing villages.

The scenery changes from the bare valley above Kingussie to the famous Insh marshes before Loch Insh, to a narrower and wooded valley for most of the river's length, and finally shingle islands on the run to the sea.

The Spey can easily be paddled in two and a half days in medium water from Kincraig, although taking three or four days makes for a more relaxed holiday.

Suggested itineraries

1. Loch Insh (accommodation) to Aviemore (campsite) – 11km.

   Aviemore to Blacksboat (campsite, booked in advance) – 35km.

   Blacksboat to Spey Bay (campsite) – 40km.

2. Loch Insh (accommodation) to Boat of Balliefurth – 31.5km.

   Balliefurth to Craigellachie campsite – 35.5km.

   Craigellachie to Spey Bay – 29km.

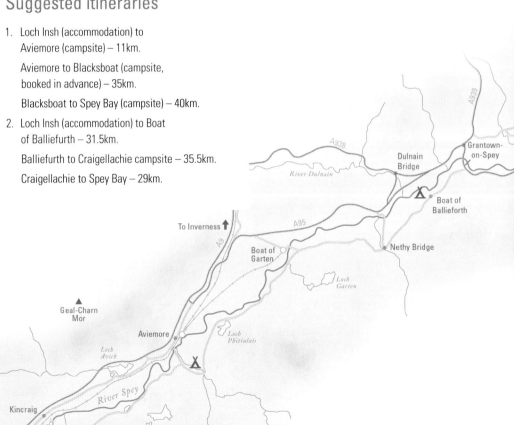

River Spey

Water level

The Spey is practically always paddleable, but a view of the river at either Kincraig or Aviemore bridge will give a good indication of the water level.

Access & egress

Possible access or egress points at:

- Loch Insh Watersports Centre on the east side of Loch Insh, reached by crossing the Spey at Kincraig on the B9152 (838 045)
- Aviemore (894 116)
- Boat of Garten (946 191)
- Broomhill Bridge (998 224), near Nethy Bridge village
- Boat of Balliefurth campsite (013 245)
- Grantown bridge (034 268)
- Cromdale bridge (066 289)
- Advie bridge (120 354)
- Ballindalloch, at a new launching point (170 369)
- Blacksboat bridge (184 390)
- Knockando (191 416)
- Carron bridge (225 411)
- Charlestown of Aberlour (262 429)
- Craigellachie (286 451)
- Boat o' Brig (318 516)
- Fochabers bridge (341 596)
- Spey Bay (349 656).

Campsites

There are campsites at Spey Bridge (Newtonmore) – (709 980), Loch Insch Watersports Centre, Aviemore, Coylumbridge, Boat of Balliefurth, Boat o' Fiddich, Craigellachie and at Spey Bay. Blacksboat camping is on flat ground at the former rail station; there is only a cold water tap.

Description

The watersports centre at Loch Insh has comfortable facilities, with a restaurant, bar and accommodation.

The Spey leaves Loch Insh under the road bridge, and glides fast down a wooded valley. After just over a kilometre, the Feshie enters from the right in a maze of islands, channels and trees, a far cry from its whitewater character higher up the glen.

The first 11km bring you to Aviemore bridge with access on the left after the bridge. The town is also on the left bank. The nearest campsite is 2km along the B970 towards Coylumbridge.

The river now slows as it meanders across a plain to Grantown, with Boat of Garten the first village after another 12km. Access to the village is on the left, and there is a useful island just below the bridge if a quieter stop is wanted. The good news is that if heading for the Boat of Balliefurth campsite you are more than halfway. This is worth remembering as the next stretch can be a bit tedious, with a long, slow, almost interminable slog, often against a wind, until Balliefurth is reached.

The campsite is near where the River Dulnain joins from the left, there is a series of standing stones on the left bank. Balliefurth is on the right bank and there is a welcome sign indicating the landing point and a field for camping with a tap and toilet in the farmyard at the back. The proprietors will come and find you for payment.

The intrepid paddler has now completed just slightly more than a third of the river but the fastest water is to come!

The next day and a few kilometres' paddling brings Grantown, the largest town in the area, set back some distance on the left from the river. This is a major crossing, you will have passed over the bridge if you did a vehicle shuttle.

Some rocks in the river warn of an approaching long rapid, which in the days of canvas canoes was a major obstacle. It is grade 2 and can be easily inspected. After this the river valley closes in for the middle part of the Spey and is mostly wooded. The next 19km, a good half-day paddle, has fast water and easy rapids, with landmarks and bridges at Cromdale and Advie. The latter has been the location for one of the first confrontations with a landowner since the advent of the Scottish Outdoor Access Code, with an access/egress point retained. Near the end of this section but before the Ballindalloch access point, there is a series of islands amongst lush wooded scenery, where there is the possibility of wild camping. It's also a part of the river where low summer water levels can mean wading.

The old Ballindalloch railway bridge signals a major access point, a few yards downriver, and a change in the character of the Spey. The next 17km provide a great and fast day trip on

continuously interesting water. On this section you might come across large groups from schools and outdoor centres.

Around the corner, the River Avon ('Ayon') joins from the right, and the river speeds up markedly. Blacksboat rapid follows, known as 'the Washing Machine' and various other names, a ramp between shingle banks, perfectly capable of filling an open canoe even in medium water. Blacksboat bridge is next, with camping on the left bank at the old railway station.

Rapids follow in quick succession, a pleasant experience. The chimney at Knockando distillery soon becomes visible with bends and an island. The middle channel of Knockand Rapid is usually taken, with the drop very near to the left bank at the end. Immediately after, steps lead up to an SCA car park. In the next 4km there are five rapids, all straightforward with obvious channels, large waves in high water, down a scenic wooded valley to Carron, another distillery.

About halfway down between Carron and Aberlour is the last rapid of this series, with an appreciable drop. Aberlour is very obvious, a sprawling village on the right bank with a flat grass open space. The river winds around Aberlour, a long shallow right-hand bend. More than 3km down is Craigellachie old bridge, followed by the new road bridge. This signals the landing, after quite a long rapid, for Boat o' Fiddich campsite on the right bank. Vehicles can be left across the road from the landing near to toilets. There is a little over 25km now to the end at the sea! Craigellachie has pubs and hotels, and Aberlour is just up the road.

The last half day brings different scenery, with the wooded bulk of Ben Aigan dominating the scene on the right bank. The valley opens up and the wide flat banks aid the salmon anglers. The Spey changes to very easy shingle rapids, but just before Boat O' Brig there are two sudden drops.

After the bridge, the right bank changes suddenly to dramatic red cliffs, known as the 'Seven Pillars of Hercules'. There are good stopping places on islands down this stretch which gives the impression of being miles from civilisation. Where power lines cross the river there is a viewpoint from the minor road high above. Fochabers, on the main A96 Aberdeen to Inverness road, is only 3km away. The village is near when a park appears rather suddenly on the right bank, followed by a bridge. The landing is below the bridge amongst trees and can be reached by a track off the minor road to Spey Bay. The village is some distance away to the right.

The final stretch of this magnificent river is different again, a flat landscape of whin bushes, gravel banks and many islands. After a weaving course amongst undergrowth and little channels, a footbridge, formerly a railway bridge, appears. One last kilometre and the very short estuary arrives suddenly, with civilisation on the right bank and the sea ahead. The car park is on the right bank near the Tugnet ice house, visitor centre, café and museum. At most times of the year there will be visitors and spectators looking at the scenery, the birds, and dolphins in the Moray Firth.

There is a campsite half a kilometre to the right of the Spey Bay Hotel. The hotel has been known to keep an eye on paddlers cars while they were completing the river. This is a good place to end a great trip.

Additional information

More detailed information can be found in the *River Spey Canoe Guide* by Nancy Chambers, also published by Pesda Press.

Eurasian badger *(Meles meles)*

The badger is the largest carnivore in the UK, and the second largest native mammal after the deer. Badgers are far more common in Scotland, than might be expected and inhabit an amazing variety of places, from coastal sand dunes to mountain crags.

They are clever, adaptable creatures, and great engineers. Badger setts, easy to distinguish by their size and shape, are found along many rivers, and between Aviemore and Boat of Garten you may visit the Strathspey Badger Hide on summer evenings.

Badger setts are large interlocking series of tunnels and chambers, they flood at times so always have an escape route to higher ground. Setts are sometimes shared with foxes, rabbits, and occasionally a visiting otter.

Badgers may be seen at twilight and after dark, so staying quiet when camping on riverbanks improves your chances of seeing them. Watching a badger sett, especially in spring when cubs come above ground for the first time, is an unforgettable experience.

08 River Dee

OS Sheets 43, 44, 37 & 38 | **Braemar to Aberdeen** | **100km**

Shuttle	58 miles, 1 hr 20-40 minutes, via A93 all the way.
Portages	Inspect and possibly portage the grade 2-3 rapids at Invercauld, Dinnet, and between Potarch and Banchory.
Start	△ Braemar, at several spots (125 907) (143 914), or at Invercauld bridge (186 900).
Finish	◎ Aberdeen boathouse bridge (943 050).

Introduction

The Dee is a major river, flowing to the sea at Aberdeen, Scotland's third city. It probably carries the least water of the country's main watercourses so has shallow shingle banks for most of the summer. However, if paddled in the spring or autumn after rain, the Dee provides a delightful trip down a mostly lightly populated valley. Little infringes on the river which is quiet and unspoilt. 'Royal Deeside' carries the cachet of Queen Victoria who loved this valley. You will pass Balmoral Castle in the upper valley, it does not dominate as it is hidden by trees.

The Dee rises on the Lairig Ghru, the major pass in the Cairngorms to the west of Ben Macdui, and flows south and then east to Braemar, famous for its Highland Games in the summer, and near the ski slopes of Glenshee to the south, on the border with Angus. The scenery in the upper stretches is of mountains with pine forests, heather moors and bouldery river banks. With snow-clad peaks well into spring, there is a northern feel to the trip, which reminds me of Norway or Canada.

Water level

The Dee is often a shallow, gravelly river, with many shallow minor rapids. It is easy to view from the A93 running up the valley. The rapid above the bridge at Potarch is a convenient point to view and assess the general state of the river.

Campsites

There are, very conveniently, campsites at Ballater and Banchory to give a superb three-day trip, but groups have taken as long as four days, and rough camping is possible in many places. As the valley is open there is plenty of parking near the river. Three days would split the river into lengths of 33, 40 and 29km.

Access & egress

Possible access or egress points at:

- Braemar (125 907)
- Invercauld bridge (186 900)
- Ballater bridge (372 956)
- Dinnet bridge (461 981)
- Aboyne bridge (523 979)
- Potarch bridge (608 973)
- Banchory bridge (698 952)
- Crathes bridge (752 957)
- Peterculter bridge (858 003)
- Bridge of Dee (928 035)
- Boathouse bridge (943 050).

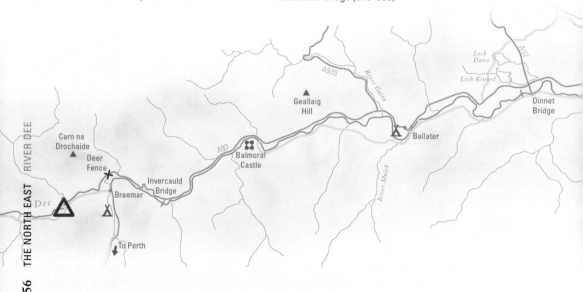

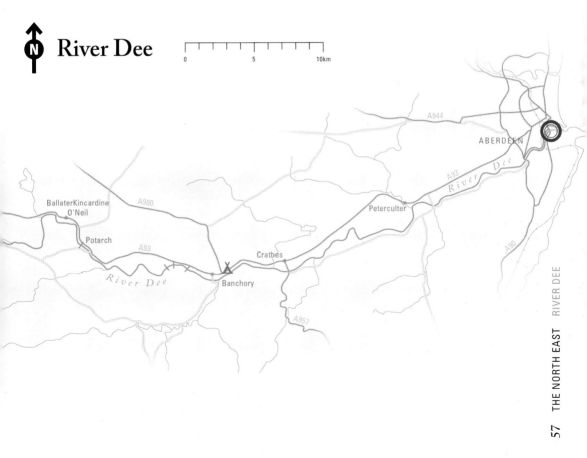

River Dee

0   5   10km

Ballater Kincardine
         O'Neil

A980

Potarch

A93

River Dee

Crathes

Banchory

Peterculter

A944

A93

River Dee

ABERDEEN

A90

A957

© Potarch Rapid, River Dee | Eddie Palmer

Description

A start can be made at two places upstream of Braemar where the road is near the river, 4 miles up at Victoria bridge, or 3 miles below Braemar at Invercauld bridge. Braemar is a lively little tourist town with many visitors in the summer, who come mainly for the sights of historic Deeside, including Balmoral. Then in snowy winters skiers arrive to enjoy the Glenshee ski slopes to the south.

On this upper stretch there is a deer fence across the river, and although somewhat broken now, it is still dangerous. It is situated opposite Braemar itself. If the river looks a bit low and stony, a better start would be below Balmoral. The river in this upper stretch winds across a flat plain, picking up speed below Invercauld. As with all long rivers, the nature of the valley and the scenery changes over distance. Considering the amount of traffic making its way up the main road alongside the Dee, the settlements are surprisingly small. The first day is a pleasant 30km down to Ballater. At Invercauld there are 400m of rocky rapids that warrant inspection, and care is required with a laden open canoe. As the Dee flows down a broad valley, inspecting the river is always easy and there are no hidden gorges to make life difficult.

Crathie bridge is the main landmark on this stretch, as Balmoral will remain hidden behind trees. The river is swollen by the River Gairn joining from the left, and the River Muick from the right.

Ballater, to the left of the river, has the first campsite, shops and hotels and is an obvious 'model village', well laid out and neat.

The second day is 40km, a good paddle for a touring trip but if the river is high enough to enjoy the rapids the water will be fast. There are rapids in the first and last thirds of the day, with a slower part in the middle.

Soon after the start, when the river narrows and speeds up, you will arrive at Cambus O' May, the name of a long right-hand bend with fast water, turbulent around the bridge arches and which makes large waves in high water. There is a Victorian footbridge here and a hotel on the left bank over the road. The riverside became a popular walking destination in Victorian times after Balmoral was built for Queen Victoria. She made Deeside the Costa Brava of its day!

Rapids build up gradually after this and just above Dinnet bridge is a large rocky rapid worth inspecting. A landing can be made on the right bank and there is a track heading up diagonally to the road amongst the trees. The bridge itself is high above the river and awkward to access.

The Dee then quietens down for a few miles and Aboyne is the halfway mark for this day's paddling. The village is to the left with egress downstream of the bridge. This is still a quiet area and Aboyne is the first of the commuter villages for Aberdeen. A further 12km of quiet-ish paddling with large islands downstream of Aboyne lead past Kincardine O' Neil to Potarch bridge, with a steep rapid just above the bridge. There is a good landing and car parking up the bank on the left side of the main road where you are likely to meet anglers. The next few miles are the main fishing area on the Dee.

River Dee near Linn of Dee Bridge | Eddie Palmer

Potarch marks the beginning of the most popular canoeing stretch on the Dee, with flat water for a few kilometres and then the largest rapids on the river. The Potarch Hotel on the right bank is worth visiting.

After a long bend to the left, small rapids commence amongst pretty wooded scenery. There are many fishing platforms, croys (solid stone jetties built out into the river) and lodges for some 4km.

Cairnton rapid starts on a bend to the left and drops, leading into easy waves. It appears to be more difficult than it is and can be inspected from the left bank. Where the rapid finishes, a rocky right bank can be seen ahead, signalling the start of Invercannie. This can be inspected from the right bank and is straightforward, although it has large waves. The route is near the right bank, a steep first drop, large waves and a second drop 100m further on.

Although large waves can swamp an open canoe, this rapid is usually shot without problem. Very high water may increase the grading of Invercannie to grade 3. It is now an exhilarating paddle down to Banchory, with several artificial side walls built for angling creating nice large central waves.

The campsite at Banchory is on the left, downstream of the bridge, and the town is the largest so far coming down the river. From now on, there are easy little rapids and the countryside is much more agricultural. The river is still worth doing for these last 29km, as the valley is quiet right into Bridge of Dee at Aberdeen.

The villages on the banks, mainly the left side, are dormitory communities serving Aberdeen. Crathes, on the left bank at the first bridge is worth visiting. Drumoak, Peterculter and Miltimber follow. The right bank is mostly wooded and quiet. Bridge of Dee is recognisable by the supermarkets on the left, the setting is now urban. The trip can only continue for a further 2km as small craft are banned from Aberdeen's busy oil industry harbour. Egress is at Aberdeen Boat Club, two bridges down.

A truly intrepid voyage ... from snowy mountains down to the sea.

SKYE TO MULL | 📷 *Loch Nevis | Dave Girling*

Skye to Mull west coast favourites

An Introduction

The centre of the west coast of Scotland is spectacular ... featuring high, inaccessible mountains, offshore islands, and fjord-like long sea lochs. As a result road connections can be tortuous, reflecting the nature of the terrain, with long vehicle shuttle routes.

This is one of the truly wild areas of the country. It is possible to walk on the Knoydart peninsula without seeing any other people for two or three days, an increasingly unlikely opportunity in Britain.

Mallaig is the major ferry and fishing port on the west central coast. The 'Road to the Isles' runs from Fort William, the nearest large settlement, to Mallaig, and one of Britain's most spectacular railways follows a different route, a line often running steam trains. Mallaig is more a working town than a resort like Oban, but it gives access to Skye via the Armadale car ferry. Boat trips leave for the Small Isles and there are many other attractions nearby.

The Small Isles are four very different islands, out in the sea to the south of Skye. Sea kayakers are drawn to them, usually from Arisaig, like moths to a flame. Arisaig, to the south of Mallaig, has several campsites, some of them seasonal, and many white sandy beaches.

Muck is the smallest and most southerly, it still supports crofting and a small population. It is one of the few parts of Britain where manual labour in the tiny fields can still be seen. At the small harbour of Port Mor is one of the most comfortable phone boxes in the UK, with a chair and cushion, and often a vase of flowers.

Eigg to the north has 'won its independence' through a community buy-out under Scottish legislation. It now has a new harbour, a car ferry, community businesses and accommodation to let, a far cry from life under previous landlords.

Rhum, the largest of the Small Isles, further out in the Sea of the Hebrides, is a national nature reserve, with world-famous research into the life and habits of the red deer population living there. Spectacular mountains rise straight out of the sea.

The furthest out from the mainland is Canna, with a safe and good anchorage, making it a common stop-over for yachtsmen on their way out to the Western Isles. Canna is in the care of the National Trust for Scotland and has several families living there.

To the west of Fort William, the large, rugged peninsulas of Ardgour and Morvern stick out into the sea, most easily reached by the car ferry at Corran. Although a very short ride over Loch Linnhe, arriving in Ardgour by ferry adds a bit of spice. Many choose to travel to Mull by driving through this barren landscape and then taking the ferry between Lochaline and Fishnish.

© Glenfinnan Monument and Loch Shiel | Dave Walsh

09 Loch Hourn

OS Sheet 33 | **Kinloch Hourn to Arnisdale** | **27km**

Shuttle	It is best to paddle out and return, because the one-way route, via Glen Garry, the A87, and the Glenelg road, is some 56 miles, and almost two hours long!
Start	△ Kinloch Hourn (950 070).
Finish	○ Arnisdale (845 105), or back at Kinloch Hourn.

Introduction

After a long drive over a twisting road, and a precipitous drop down a hill to Kinloch Hourn, a long fjord opens out, tempting the paddler to just get on the water and explore. This is the main entry to Knoydart, and the paddle is considerably easier than the walk down the south side of the loch. Loch Hourn is a long fjord in very remote country, with superb views of the surrounding mountains, including Ladhar Bheinn and Luinne Bheinn. The other access is by road around the northern peninsula from Glenelg to Arnisdale, from where a ferry runs over to Barrisdale Bay in the summer.

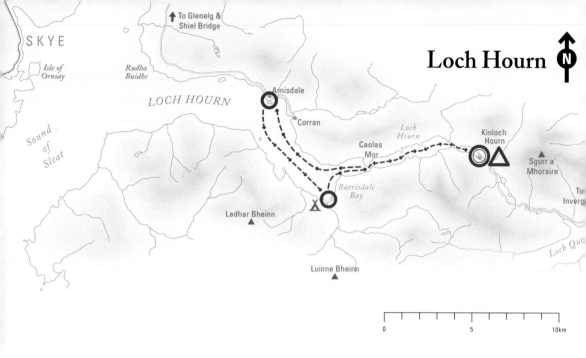

Access & egress

The only access by public road is at the start and finish. Kinloch Hourn has a large car park suitable for leaving vehicles for days. It is reached along a tortuous single-track road from Glen Garry to the east, with many steep hills and very awkward bends. The only other access for those on foot is by ferry to Barrisdale Bay (86 40).

Campsites

There is plenty of rough camping on Knoydart, and a bothy and campsite at Barrisdale Bay.

Description

Loch Hourn starts with a seaweed-filled head and continues to a first narrowing where the high sides partially block out the view ahead. The surrounding mountains often make the area feel dark, even in summer. The tides are swift in the loch, especially at the narrows. The main consideration is Caolas Mor where the water is squeezed by the long shingle spit coming out from the right (north) shore. Here the tide swirls very fast and paddling against it would be difficult. If you are planning to land at Barrisdale Bay with a fully loaded canoe or kayak, you will want to reach the bay at high tide, when a landing can be made near the campsite, requiring only a short portage. Coming through Caolas Mor near to high tide makes sense.

High and Low Water in Loch Hourn are roughly 1 hour before both HW and LW Portree.

Once through Caolas Mor, Barrisdale Bay opens out on the left side. The track which walkers take undulates along the left bank the whole way.

You might decide to just stay at Barrisdale, and even if you are not a walker or climber, a walk of some sort in this area really is called for. It is a fairly strenuous, but straightforward walk of 12km through the hills to Inverie on Loch Nevis, a village without roads, but with a well-known pub popular with yachtsmen.

If you can tear yourself away, it is a 6km paddle out to the north shore, past the hamlet of Corran to Arnisdale, from where a ferry runs to Barrisdale in the summer. This part will feel more exposed, and care is required in a strong westerly wind.

From Barrisdale Bay, the jewel in the crown is Ladhar Bheinn (pronounced 'Larven') which rises majestically in the west. It is a breathtaking mountain, with a circular route, and one of the best ridge walks in Britain. The view from the top helps understand the geography and topography of the area. To the south of Barrisdale are the other major peaks of Luinne Bheinn ('Luneven') and Meall Buidhe ('MyellBooee'). Any walk around the shattered rock, dips and gullies of this area will convince you that it is not known as 'The Rough Bounds of Knoydart' for nothing!

I remember vividly my first visit here, by canoe out to Barrisdale Bay. The following three days were spent walking and climbing in often torrential rain, though when the clouds parted on the high ridges, the views were fabulous. It was definitely on a par with Norway, Canada and some parts of Africa, for sheer desolation and loneliness. The campsite and bothy at Barrisdale were lively and interesting, with visitors from all over Europe, like us, delighting in the area and scenery.

The claim of this being an unspoilt area is not made lightly … it has been voted for by many of our European neighbours.

Knoydart

Many people have heard of Knoydart as the last great wilderness area in Great Britain, only accessible by boat, or a twenty mile walk.

The area is now within the control of the Knoydart Foundation, which finally achieved ownership of most of the old estate in 1999, after years of campaigning and action. This murky history, involving businessmen who attempted to buy in, but then left suddenly, is explained on the website of the Foundation at www.knoydart-foundation.com

The partnership includes the local community, Highland Council, the John Muir Trust, Kilchoan estate, and the Chris Brasher Trust. The foundation now guards 17,000 acres of some of the wildest land in Britain, manages properties, a bunkhouse, the deer, and generates and supplies electricity locally. It has refurbished the hydro scheme, created a small display area, and has many other projects it wishes to develop in the future.

The pub in Inverie, the Old Forge, is open every day of the year except Christmas day. It has nine moorings for boats, and provides food all day. Music is popular and is often played by the pub's visitors, so there is a chance to be part of a ceilidh every night.

There is bed and breakfast accommodation, self-catering cottages, and boat hire in Inverie. An internet search on Knoydart will give details of available accomodation as well as the boats which ply between Mallaig and Inverie.

10 Lochs Morar & Nevis

OS Sheet 40 | **Morar to Tarbet, Loch Nevis, Inverie and Mallaig** | 29km

Shuttle	Mallaig back to Morar on the A830, only 3.5 miles. If stranded at Inverie, there is a ferry back to Mallaig.
Portages	1km at Tarbet, over a track.
Start	△ Morar village (689 929).
Finish	○ Inverie (765 995) or Mallaig (678 968).

Introduction

Loch Nevis is a fabulous sea loch surrounded by mountains. It is infamous for very strong local winds coming down from the mountains. It can be reached without a canoe by passenger ferry from Mallaig to Inverie, which is worth visiting in its own right.

Loch Morar is more sheltered than the sea lochs to the north. It is a lovely west coast loch, separated from the sea by the sands of the very short River Morar and the main road to Mallaig.

This is a fine trip in great scenery which can be quite safe if you pay close attention to conditions on LochNevis. You could easily spend a week in this area.

Looking east down Loch Morar | Dave Walsh

Access & egress

This is a committing trip, with paddling out being the normal 'escape route'. The only road access is at Morar or Mallaig.

Campsites

The nearest formal sites are south towards Arisaig, on a lovely stretch of coast (six sites at the last count, some of which may only take caravans). There are plenty of rough sites along Loch Morar and Loch Nevis.

Description

Loch Morar stretches away to high mountains, and attracts the eye to its end, where a watershed leads walkers over to Glen Dessary and Glen Pean, and thence to Loch Arkaig and the Great Glen.

Islands in the first part of Loch Morar break up the scenery. A road follows the north shore for 4km to the pier at Bracorina, and after a further 3km is Brinacory Island. It is then 4km to the way over to Loch Nevis, or 7km more to the end of the loch, if a diversion for isolated walking and camping is desired.

As with all large Scottish lochs, the wind can blow hard, but will usually be from the west and behind you. Crossing the loch entails a 2km paddle that could be hard, so in windy conditions it is advised to follow the north shore.

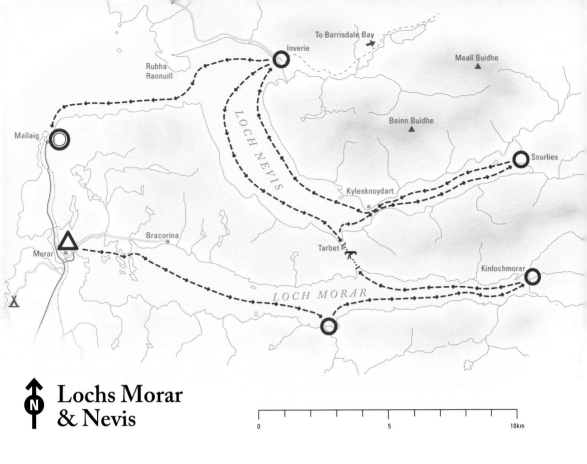

Lochs Morar & Nevis

0   5   10km

The way into Loch Nevis is by a portage along the track from South Tarbet Bay over to Tarbet, it is just over 1km and not too rough (track with stones). On the Loch Nevis side there is a chapel converted into a bothy, and camping is available.

You must now make a decision, east or west? Paddling east for 8km will bring you through the narrows of Kylesknoydart to the sandy beaches around the islands of Eilean Maol and Eilean Tioram, and the head of another loch with great scenery. Intrepid yachtsmen sometimes make their way up here. Sourlies Bothy lies in the southern arm of the head, where there is access to the watershed at Sgurr na Ciche, and the way over to the dam at the head of Loch Quoich.

The paddle west from Tarbet is down an ever-widening loch to Inverie, the centre of the Knoydart district. For a village with no access road, Inverie is a lively place, a great favourite of west coast sailors, a target for walkers, who often return to Mallaig using the ferry. The pub and restaurant are famous, and the little tourist information centre (with internet access of course) stays open late!

If a day is taken reaching Tarbet along Loch Morar, a further three or four days could easily be taken in fetching up at Inverie, due to all the diversions along the way.

The return could be made the same way of course, but a different route, with more risk, is to return by sea to Mallaig, which is 9.5km.

Loch Nevis has to be crossed at some point. One choice is to hug the north shore around to the headland of Rubha Raonuill, with its obvious monument and then cross directly over the busy sea route to the rugged south shore. Alternatively, one can cross directly from Inverie to the south shore off Sgeir a Ghaill.

By hugging the sheltered south side, with the tide and no head wind, you will get to Mallaig in about two hours. The weather should be calm and settled.

Whichever way you choose, this is a great west coast journey.

The Highland clearances

In the Scottish Highlands, 'the clearances' is the name given to a planned and often brutal forced land clearance, which began in the 1760s.

The clearances came about because of agricultural change. Although all of the UK was subject to something similar, it was the lack of any legal protection for highland tenants, the rapidity of change for the clan system, and the sheer brutality that marked these clearances out.

Forced displacement of the people meant that they were driven out of their homes, often only given a short time to collect possessions before their houses were burned. People, often whole extended families, were then on the road as vagrants. In the often harsh weather conditions, the young and elderly could die in misery outside their houses or on the side of the road.

Many made their way to ports, and emigrated. The rest ended up in crofting townships on the very edge of any fertile land, becoming more or less slave labour for landlords in such activities as kelp harvesting.

However, the clearance of clans was not the sole domain of absentee English landlords. Many of those responsible were Scots, who had taken up cattle droving, become rich, and land owners, and saw themselves as landlords.

The Jacobite Risings lead to repeated government efforts to curb the clans. After the Battle of Culloden in 1746, clans were suppressed ruthlessly, and supportive small agricultural townships disappeared, leading to the abandoned glens seen all over the west coast.

Elizabeth Gordon, the 19th Countess of Sutherland, and her factor, were particularly cruel. The people of Sutherland have not forgiven the family to this day. An account by Donald McLeod runs:

"The consternation and confusion were extreme. Little or no time was given for the removal of persons or property; the people striving to remove the sick and the helpless before the fire should reach them; next, struggling to save the most valuable of their effects. The cries of the women and children, the roaring of the affrighted cattle, hunted at the same time by the yelling dogs of the shepherds amid the smoke and the fire, altogether presented a scene that completely baffles description ... it required to be seen to be believed."

© Glenfinnan Viaduct | VisitScotland/ScottishViewpoint

11 Loch Shiel Circuit

 **OS Sheet 40 | Glenfinnan to Lochailort | 60km**

Shuttle	Glenfinnan to Loch Ailort along the A830 only 10 miles, 15 minutes
Portages	Possible portage of the one grade 2 rapid on the River Shiel. Parts of Loch Moidart at low tide.
Start	△ Glenfinnan hotel pier (901 805).
Finish	○ Lochailort jetty (759 814).

Introduction

The area is well known for both longer expeditions, and a unique 'round trip', probably the second-most frequent canoe trip undertaken in Scotland. The loch is a wilderness experience, with no roads for most of its 30km length, from Glenfinnan, the famous monument on the 'Road to the Isles', at the north end, to Acharacle at the southern end. Wildlife is plentiful; otters, pine martens, golden eagles, and if you are very lucky, wild cats.

A short river adds variety and Loch Moidart offers various options, including a fairly easy sea loch, an estuary, and a round-the-coast trip with reasonably easy escapes.

This is a fantastically varied journey through inland and coastal scenery in a beautiful and unspoilt area of Scotland.

Access & egress

Access is possible at the north end, at the hotel (901 805) at Glenfinnan. At Acharacle, access/egress can be difficult. The pier on the left (east) side at Acharacle is used by commercial boats, and there is almost no parking. A better egress is just after the bridge, entering the River Shiel, on the left bank. All the roads in the area are narrow, with limited parking; A860 at Glenuig (674 777), A861 along Loch Ailort (various places over 4km), Lochailort village (768 824).

The head of Loch Moidart at Ardmorlich pier on the A861 (697 728) is often dry. It is better to travel down to Castle Tioram (663 724), a ruin reached down the road running alongside the River Shiel from Shiel Bridge. There is a car park at the end, used by walkers, and people who come to stare at the castle, which is crumbling away due to arguments between its owner and the conservation authorities.

Water level

The River Shiel can be shallow and gravelly in dry weather. A good idea of the level can be gained from looking over Shiel Bridge, or just below it.

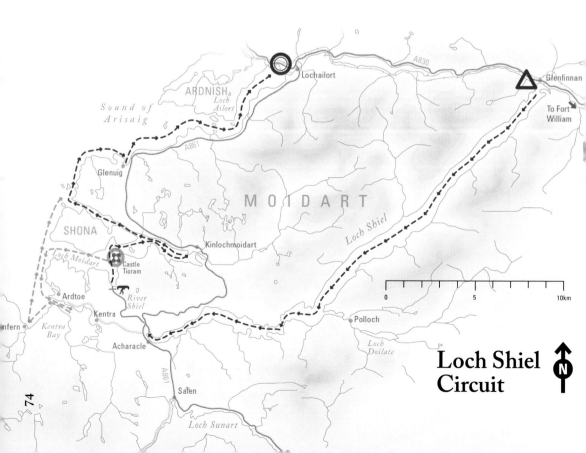

Campsites

The nearest formal site is at Resipole on Loch Sunart. Wild camping is possible in many places down Loch Shiel (in summer, shingle spits are best to avoid midges), on the islands in Loch Moidart (be careful to avoid being near houses), and on the islands in both North and South Channels. There are also suitable places on the shores of Loch Ailort.

Description

The scenery is superb all the way down. Small islands become much more frequent about halfway down. The first large bay is 20km down the loch, on the left where the River Polloch comes in. Polloch village is situated 1km inland from the end of the inlet. At Polloch it is possible to egress onto a road, which is very tortuous and leads to Strontian on Loch Sunart.

Two kilometres further on at the narrows is the well-known burial ground island, Eilean Fhianain, and St Firman's Chapel. The left bank then opens out into Claish Moss, a large bog, and Acharacle follows after a further 6km.

The River Shiel becomes obvious at the end of the loch, with Shiel Bridge the only bridge. The river is only 3.5km long, and has had nuisance anglers in the past, especially at the bottom, where a sizeable rapid spills into the sea at low tide. The river is narrow all the way down, with fishing platforms and other detritus sticking out into the channel.

Launching will always be possible on Loch Moidart at Castle Tioram (pronounced 'Churram'). Then the glories of Shona Beag, Eilean Shona and a couple of smaller islands can be experienced. If starting from Castle Tioram this is a 14km short round trip.

From North Channel it is a 5km sea voyage around to the village of Glenuig, the latter part is sheltered by Samalaman Island. This headland is exposed in bad weather. Glenuig has a famous and lively village hall, with music offered in the summer season, and a small community shop. Glenuig Inn is paddler friendly, offers good food and accomodation, a bunkhouse, camping on the foreshore, sea kayak hire and a shuttle service.

The coast is somewhat bare for the next 3km untill islands offer some shelter. The main road is always present on the right-hand side. Roshven has a beach, and then Loch Ailort offers a narrow sea loch and shelter all the way for 7km to the beach and jetty at the head of the loch.

Variation

If feeling brave, there is a wothwhile expedition to the south from Castle Tioram: go out of South Channel, turn left at Farquhar's Point, paddle some 2.5km around to Ardtoe (628 708), and you will find a delightful spot with beautiful sandy beaches. Inland from here is Kentra, an interesting area of little creeks, when the tide is high enough to provide water to float your canoe. Then, 2.5km further south-west from Ardtoe is Gortenfern (612 691), and another fabulous beach, also reached by a walk from Arivegaig.

Pine martens (*Martes martes*)

Pine martens are commonly found in this area, although rarely seen in daylight. They are famous for appearing at the holiday cottages near Loch Teacuis off Loch Sunart but are almost unknown to many visitors to Scotland. They appear at first sight rather like a short-legged cat with a bushy tail. The pine marten is a lithe creature, good at climbing, and often found on Scots pine. It has rich brown fur and a creamy yellow throat, and is most often seen either bounding across a forest ride, or leaping from stone to stone on the shore, or across a burn. It can swim, but prefers not to.

Martens of all types (Europe has a stone marten, *Martes foina*) have a sweet tooth, and can be tempted by such fare as jam sandwiches. They are leading characters in the books by Mike Tomkies, author and naturalist, who lived for several years on the west shore of Loch Shiel. He became frustrated by people trying to find out where he lived, and then coming to disturb his studies. Mike wished to get closer to wildlife, especially golden eagles and wild cats. As well as rescuing wild cat kittens and bringing them up, he made friends with a group of pine martens, who came to feed each night at his cottage. Eventually, he moved to the mountains in northern Spain to get more peace and quiet.

12 Loch Sunart

OS Sheets 40 & 49 | Resipole to Strontian & Glenborrowdale | 44km

Shuttle	Parking at Resipole avoids long and slow drives along the side of Loch Sunart; from Strontian down to Glenborrowdale would be 21km and about 45 minutes.
Start/Finish	△ ◯ Resipole campsite (725 640).

Introduction

This loch is one of the longest and most interesting sea lochs in Scotland. The inland end is very sheltered, making it a useful destination if the weather is too wild out at sea. The road along the north side provides access to the Ardnamurchan peninsula, a place worth visiting in its own right. It is one of the most tortuous and slow roads in the country, and not to be tackled with a caravan or trailer unless absolutely necessary. This area cries out for a central base, and Resipole provides one. The campsite, east of Salen, gives access to beaches on Ardnamurchan, the whole of Loch Sunart, Loch Shiel to the north, and Loch Teacuis on the south side. The description covers Loch Teacuis eastwards, as the outer loch is very open to weather coming in from the west.

Access & egress

The north side of Loch Sunart has a road all the way along it, the A861 as far as Salen, and then the B8007, which eventually winds its way to Ardnamurchan Point. Access is possible at Strontian (815 615), Resipole farm and landing (725 640), Salen (690 648), a useful picnic site and car park (680 630) and, with some difficulty, near the Glenborrodale Hotel (620 606). However, all of the roads are narrow, mostly single-track, and can be extremely congested in summer. Care is especially required with trailers.

Campsites & accommodation

Resipole campsite is well-situated, with space for tents, caravans, and camper vans. It has cabins for rent, as well as a bar and restaurant. There is one other small site at Strontian.

Description

The recommended start is from Resipole, however as it is at the centre of the loch I will describe the area from west to east. You can park at Resipole without staying there, but parking is limited on the roadside.

The prevailing tide and wind in the outer reaches of the loch are from the west. Access at the west end of the loch is from the Ardnamurchan road, around Glenborrodale on the north side. Parking is scarce in this area, but the owner of the hotel east of Glenborrodale has allowed paddlers to use his jetty, and there is parking at the hotel.

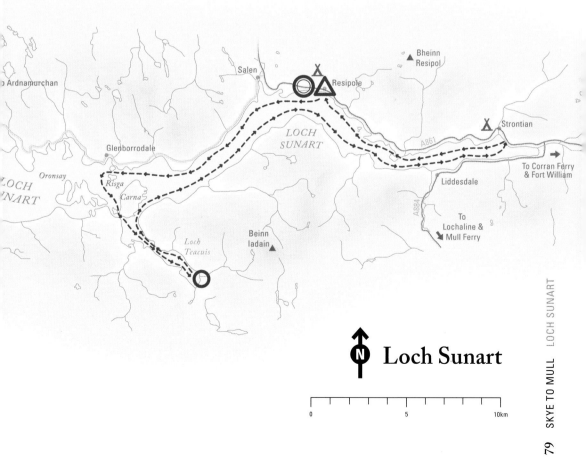

Bheinn
Resipol ▲

Salen

To Ardnamurchan

Resipole

Strontian

LOCH
SUNART

A861

Glenborrodale

To Corran Ferry
& Fort William

Oronsay

Risga

LOCH
UNART

Carna

Liddesdale

A884

To
Lochaline &
Mull Ferry

Loch
Teacuis

Beinn
Iadain ▲

N

Loch Sunart

0   5   10km

The route is down the west side of Carna. If there is a stong west wind cross to the east of Risga and Carna, as this reduces the exposed crossing to a minimum. This gives access to Loch Teacuis through the narrow western passage. The tide runs very fast, so enter preferably near the top of the flood (as the tide is coming up to High Water). HW Salen is up to 15 minutes either side of HW Oban. Loch Teacuis is one of the most unspoilt small sea lochs on the west coast, and worth making the effort to see. It is 5km long, and feels wild and isolated, although there are holiday cottages here. There are also a few campsites, but the midges are bad in summer.

The east passage between Carna and the mainland is wider, and has two reefs in its entrance. These are no problem for a canoeist, whether paddling or sailing.

From Carna to Salen village is 9km. There is a Forestry Commission picnic site and car park on the left bank, just before Salen, which is extremely convenient for launching. Resipole campsite is 3.5km further on, and the Ben Resipole mountain path leaves at the back of the campsite.

Opposite Resipole , there are some small islets, with lots of seals and occasionally otters. From Resipole up to 'The Narrows', at Glas Eilean, is 5km, with interesting islands on the left side, otter habitat, and plenty of landing and picnic sites away from the road. The narrow part has strong tides. The right (south) side of the loch, at first steep-sided and wooded, becomes estate land with holiday homes.

From Glas Eilean to Strontian village is a sheltered 6km, and at low tide, there is much mud and sand off Strontian, with a risk of grounding on an ebb tide. The mooring buoys on the left side are for guests at the hotel visible on the north shore. The jetty is 1km further on and has parking. You are now at the head of Loch Sunart and ahead are the mountains of Ardgour.

An interesting and scenic paddle in a wild area.

Common seals *(Phoca vitulina)*

Seals will be encountered in all of the Scottish west coast lochs. These are usually common seals, which in fact aren't common at all. Common seals appear to favour sheltered inner lochs. They have 'dog-like' heads and are smaller than their more numerous grey cousins.

In discussions in Scotland with regard to a 'Marine Watching Code', some naturalists, who presumably had never put to sea in a small boat, held the belief that kayaking is a problem for seals. Experienced paddlers will know that seals often swim up to non-powered craft as they are very curious. For those who regularly holiday and paddle on the west coast, seals are a natural part of the scenery. 'Boat trips to see Seals!' notices bring a wry smile to my lips – as if there was any risk of not seeing seals! The local boatman has of course done his homework, and knows that the same seals will be seen on the same rock skerries every day. As soon as the tide drops in the daytime, seals haul themselves out to lie and sleep in the sun.

Whether in a kayak or canoe, seals will usually come up for a peep behind you, as if to make sure that this large yellow or green thing is real. They will often hang around to see what will happen. It is not unusual in shallow water for seals to swim underneath craft time after a time … they are not frightened.

At the Scottish Canoe Association's annual exhibition, trade fair, and general get-together, held in Perth every October, there is a photographic competition for paddlers. A few of years ago, a winning photograph was of a baby seal who had hauled itself out onto the back deck of a sea kayak.

Majestic Mountains

An Introduction

This awe-inspiring part of west central Scotland is bounded by Fort William to the north, and Oban to the west, with Tyndrum and Crianlarich at the centre. It includes one of the finest sea lochs, one of the largest inland lochs, and two fine overland routes.

This area now looks as if it has always been deserted, with few signs of agriculture. However in the 17th and 18th centuries the southern highlands were highly populated, with fertile *straths* (broad valleys) growing crops to support the people and grazing for cattle. Moorland and conifers have replaced the fields and woods of past centuries.

The journey from Tyndrum over bleak Rannoch Moor and into Glencoe is as spectacular as ever, with the view westwards eventually alighting upon the west coast, and the mountains of Ardgour beyond.

Glencoe is forever associated with the massacre which took place in 1692, distinctive in the history of clan bloodshed. The Highlands have seen many massacres over the centuries, often arguments over the ownership of cattle, or of cattle-grazing rights. The MacGregors massacred 140 Colquhouns in Glen Fruin, west of Loch Lomond; the Clan Donald once burnt to death hundreds of Campbells in a barn near Oban; more than a hundred Lamonts were executed at Dunoon in revenge for changing sides after the Battle of Inverlochy near Fort William.

However, the Glencoe massacre was carried out by a division of the English army raised from Clan Campbell. The order was given by the then Secretary of State for Scotland, John Dalrymple, under a demand for allegiance to William of Orange from pro-Jacobite clans. The Donalds were slow to accede and the popular story is that the Campbells came under cover of night to ask for refuge from winter weather. In fact the Campbells stayed for two weeks, using the usual Highland hospitality of the Donalds. The pretence for being there was the collection of the Cess Tax, a Scottish tax. The massacre was an action carried out when the Donalds had been lulled into a false sense of security. In the early morning, with all asleep, the assailants struck, and slaughtered thirty-eight men, women and children. Many of those who escaped perished on the wintery hills.

East of Tyndrum are the mountains which were the home and range of Rob Roy MacGregor, and his legacy can be found in the hills south of Loch Earn, the glens and mountains of Balquhidder, and the Trossachs to the west of Callander. Rob Roy's grave is in Balquhidder village (beware of traffic on the narrow roads in the summer), and there is a visitor centre with information about him in Callander, the 'Gateway to the Trossachs'. Rob Roy was a wronged cattle dealer, who became an outlaw and a guerrilla in a private war against the Marquess of Montrose. His life was one of daring raids and dramatic escapes from capture.

In the south-west of this area are sites of unique ancient history. West of Loch Awe is Kilmartin Glen, with cup-and-ring stones, brochs, caves, and burial grounds. This area was once highly populated as it was the gateway from Ireland by sea.

13 Across Rannoch Moor

 OS Sheets 41, 50 & 42 | Loch Ba to Rannoch Station | 13km

Shuttle	One of the longest vehicle shuttles in Scotland, about 83 miles each way, via a long triangle south and east, along the A82, A85, A827 through Killin, and B846 to Tummel Bridge, and Rannoch Station.
Portages	In low water, the first part of the trip could entail some short portages; thick mud, reeds, grassy islands and dead-ends. There are also rocky stretches of river, requiring either carrying, or lining down. At end, 0.5km from Dubh Lochan up track to Rannoch Station.
Start	△ Loch Ba, on the A82 (309 495).
Finish	◎ Dubh Lochan near Rannoch Station (415 576).

Introduction

This is another classic trip and Rannoch Moor is unforgettable. Many people have looked on the moor as a challenge. It features in early literature of intrepid expeditions, long before modern charity challenges became popular. A 1930s book on first ascents of Scottish mountains (if you don't count generations of local shepherds), features a raft trip that became literally bogged down.

Because of the height and proximity to the west coast and its weather, the climate is harsh and unsettled, bringing snow, sleet and torrential rain any time of year.

Rannoch Moor has been crossed from the far west side over to Rannoch Station, a serious expedition. The trip in this section is much shorter but just as likely to leave you soaked, if only for one day. Navigation is difficult in the flat boggy terrain, but an encircling panorama of mountains feasts the eye.

Description

This trip comes into the expedition category because high summer brings low water, lots of mud and many midges. In other seasons you might encounter snow and sleet showers. Once on the moor, there is literally no escape; it's either onwards … or back.

The main road gives access to Loch Ba, which is some 2.5km long, and heads generally north-east. It has islands, which can be quite disconcerting when trying to navigate. Once here, the sounds of the road will have disappeared and you will be on your own. In a couple of places the loch narrows, the second narrows heralds a turn of the loch to the right, and the gradual start of the River Ba. The river is not obvious, as it hardly has any flow and in certain levels of water, you risk heading down cul-de-sacs.

The river winds for several kilometres eventually flowing into Loch Laidon, which is L-shaped. Loch Laidon heads north-east in the general direction one wants to go, and has a north-westerly arm. This part of the loch enters a real wilderness, and is worth exploring, perhaps even camping on one of the islands. The general terrain is very watery. Take your time on this trip, as rarely will you be so much on your own.

Campsites

On the route, look for slightly higher ground ... everywhere is boggy. There are no formal sites nearby, apart from down in Glencoe.

Water level

On Rannoch Moor, take it as it comes. There should be some flow in the little rivers.

At the finish, there should be a good flow from Loch Laidon down the Garbh Ghaoir.

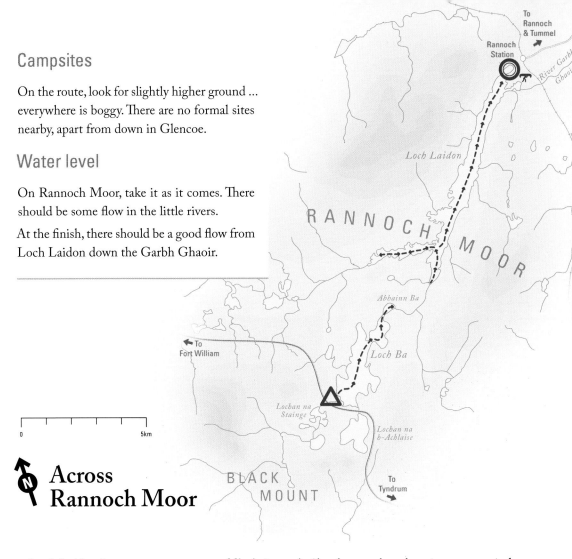

Across Rannoch Moor

Loch Laidon is not too extreme to paddle, being only 8km long, unless there is a strong wind. At least it should blow you towards Rannoch Station. The view ahead is of the mountains in the Rannoch deer forest to the north.

Near the end of Loch Laidon, avoid the Garbh Ghaoir river, which leaves to the south, as you might end up travelling rather fast in the wrong direction. At the end of the loch is a short half kilometre portage from the little Dubh Lochan up a track to Rannoch Station.

Access & egress

The start is at one of Britain's most remote and windswept points, where the A82 crosses over to Glencoe. Access Loch Ba on the east side, where a small connecting river flows under the only bridge on this road; just after a large lochan on the west side (309 495). There is only one lay-by to park in on this bit of road.

Egress is off the Dubh Lochan, north side (417 578) after Loch Laidon.

Rannoch Moor

Rannoch Moor is a triangular plateau of fifty square miles, at an altitude of just over 300m. It is subject to frequent 'driech' weather (in the Scots language), and in the novel 'Kidnapped', Robert Louis Stevenson stated "a wearier looking desert a man never saw".

The surface is dotted with innumerable lochans, streams and peat bogs, and mountains rise on all sides to over 600m, and often 1,000m. The area has a railway line, the famous West Highland line, on its eastern side, and the A82 main road from Bridge of Orchy to Fort William on its western side. Otherwise ... nothing.

Many people see in Rannoch Moor a mood influenced by the weather, and certainly the colours of the landscape change frequently. The area delights in superlatives – a scenic road, often quite frightening in winter, a popular railway line, one of the best in Europe, and a hard walk across from Rannoch Station to the Kingshouse Hotel at the top of Glencoe. There is also a fairly new route, the West Highland Way skirting the west side of the moor near the road.

The Rannoch Station area is well known to determined walkers, as it is a convenient stop-off for commencing many great walks. Train-spotters delight in being able to photo-graph locomotives in a wild setting, especially steam trains. Members of the public can be transported into a wilderness with no risk, by train or by car.

Within a fairly small country, the area to the east of the A82 road that has no other roads, is surprising and unusual.

14 Loch Etive

 OS Sheets 49 & 50 | Glen Etive to Dunstaffnage | 72km

Shuttle	Another long trip around by road, 45 miles to Connel Bridge via the A82 to Ballachulish, and A828 south, taking at least an hour.
Portages	The Falls of Lora (tidal falls) are formidable at certain states of tide.
Start	△ End of Glen Etive on the sea loch (111 454).
Finish	◎ Dunstaffnage Marina (886 339).

Introduction

Loch Etive lies between Oban and Fort William, a long tidal loch with a strong tide. The loch is used for one of the many multi-sport races, which after a bike ride from Glencoe to Bonawe Narrows, features a kayak race up the loch to its head, and a run back up Glen Etive to the start. It makes good television, with a backdrop of grand mountains.

Near the open sea, under Connel Bridge, are the Falls of Lora, a magnet for whitewater paddlers, as the falls run on every ebb tide. At high tide the rock shelf is covered, but as the water level drops the 'fall' reveals itself.

The trip features a paddle from high mountains, in a beautiful glen, to a busy sea loch entrance, with the town of Oban just around the corner at the end.

Water level

The loch is tidal and the flow is particularly fast at the narrows under Connel Bridge. It is best to do the described trip on a falling tide so that the ebb tide is flowing in your direction of travel. HW Bonawe is 2 hours 10 minutes after HW Oban (+0210) and HW Connel is 10 minutes after HW Oban (+0010).

Description

The head of the loch has a sand and shingle beach, and at some times of the year can be quite busy as lots of people camp here. Take advantage of your water transport to get away from it all, and move seawards for a first camp. As soon as you leave the road behind, noisy groups enjoying a midnight rave fade into the distance.

It is a lovely 16km down to the first egress at Bonawe Narrows, with many places to land on both banks, where burns enter the loch. There are narrow valleys to explore, and mountains to climb if the mood takes you. Few people live in this area and their access is via 4x4 tracks. The loch is mostly about half a kilometre wide, but widens to 2km halfway down.

Bonawe is flat and marshy, and the tide runs strongly through the narrows. The main settlement is on the right side, with Taynuilt village to the left, the River Awe (of whitewater fame) entering on the left, and usually many fishermen concentrating on the salmon entering the Awe. After Bonawe, the loch widens, swings to the right, and Airds Point follows after a further 3km. Fish farms become numerous, Loch Etive being a very productive fish loch, due to its scouring tides.

Access & egress

The following alternative access and egress points are reccomended:

- · Connel, north bank (909 346)
- · Achnachoich pier (961 340)
- · Airds Bay jetty, end of River Awe (011 327).

Campsites

There is a campsite at Ledaig, north of Connel and rough sites on the sides of the upper loch.

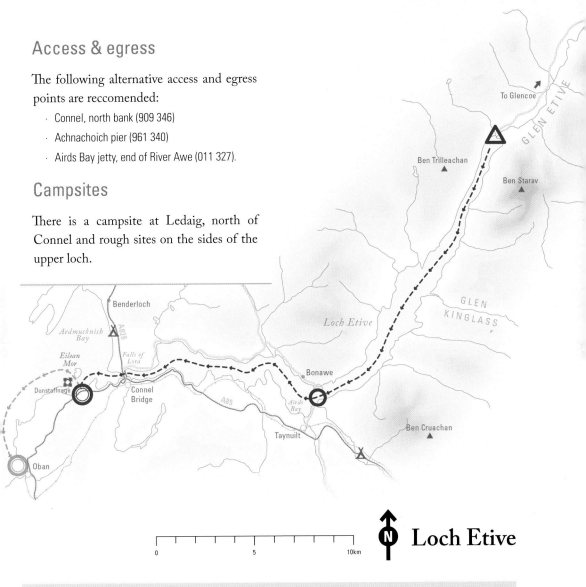

Loch Etive

Mussel farming

I was totally ignorant of the whole business of shellfish 'farming' until a distant relative started up a mussel farm on Loch Etive. The 'technical' aspects of this enterprise appear to be the need to be competent enough to build a frame to hold the mussels which will withstand winter storms, and then to 'harvest' the mussels in winter weather. After this, a market has to be found for the produce. Refrigerated trucks arrive every day to take the mussels to France and Spain.

The mussels grow all by themselves on ropes hung off a wooden frame, in salt water cleansed by a good tide. This must be one of the simplest ways of farming.

© Golden Eagle | VisitScotland/ScottishViewpoint

The loch turns west, and after another 3km, Achnachoich signals a jetty and road on the left (south) out to the main A85, with gardens to visit in the summer.

Boats and moorings then start to proliferate, and after a further 4km, the unmistakeable shape of the metal Connel Bridge appears. Under the bridge are the Falls of Lora, which run very strong at spring low tides. The main passage for boats is close to the left (south) bank. The right side has a rock ledge which uncovers, and if the tide is ebbing, there are bound to be whitewater kayaks playing on it. For an easy passage, go down on the last of the ebb.

Connel Bridge village signals the start of the Oban suburbs, and the usual egress, 2km downstream is at Dunstaffnage Marina. Take care when paddling amongst the pontoons. There is a slipway to the right of the main pontoon. Ask about parking and unloading, as the marina can be very busy in summer. There is a bar and restaurant.

Variation

In settled weather, it is possible to paddle down to Oban. Leave Loch Etive south of Eilean Mor, and hug the coast. It is only some 3km to Ganavan bay, with a road along to Oban. If going as far as Oban, it would be worthwhile planning ahead where to land and park in this very busy harbour (as several regular ferry routes terminate here). It may be a good idea to leave the water soon after entering Oban Bay, on the left side near the cathedral.

Loch Awe from Kilchrenan | Dave Walsh

15 Loch Awe

 OS Sheets 50 & 59 | **Dalmally to Ford** | **72km**

Shuttle	North to south, from near Dalmally down the east side to Ford via the A819 and the single-track B840. This is about 25 miles, and can be very slow. Allow an hour for the single journey.
Start	△ Near Kilchurn Castle, off the A85 (139 279).
Finish	◎ Ford pier (874 045).

Introduction

The loch is one of the largest in Scotland. Although the scenery, long stretches of conifers, is perhaps not to everyone's taste, it does make the loch appear quite Canadian. The area can give many days of canoeing, with the traffic on the roads on both sides invisible for most of the time. Very few other people will be encountered, only a few fishermen.

Higher up, on the west side, the much smaller Loch Avich is joined by a short river, and is another connected area to explore.

Access & egress

The loch is surprisingly difficult to access, with very few easy ways onto the water. This appears to be historical, and also deliberate, to prevent those without fishing licences getting to the water undetected. This should get better thanks to the Access Code as the Forestry Commission owns virtually all the land around. The following access and egress points are recommended:

- At the top end, below the A85 road bridge, off the track to Kilchurn Castle (139 279).
- From the B846, on the west side, at North Port (048 214).
- From Dalavich village, on the west side, behind the houses (970 126), quite good vehicle parking.
- From Ford pier at the bottom end (874 045), The gate is usually locked, but canoes can be carried over, and vehicles parked on a long passing place on the road above.

Loch Awe

N

0   5   10km

To Oban

To Tynd

Lochawe

Kilchrenan Taychreggan
             Hotel

Cladich

To
Inveraray

Loch
Avich

River
Avich

Loch
Awe

Dalavich

Ford

Loch Ederline

To Lochgilphead

Campsites

There is a commercial campsite at Bridge of Awe, the alternatives are rough sites in the forest areas. Once on the water, campsites can be found relatively easily, look for clearings in the forest. (The existing small camp and caravan sites are private ones for anglers.) The long road down the east side has very few opportunities to access the water, and passing places must not be used for car parking or camping.

Description

There are many historic sites in the area, an island burial ground and a couple of castles and crannogs on the loch. The loch stretches away south into the distance for 36km. To the north is the ever-present bulk of Ben Cruachan.

At the north end, Kilchurn Castle is worth a visit. Lochawe village has a pub, hotel and shop. The islands in the wider northern part provide a few camping spots, although you should be aware of the rough ground and midges in summer.

The long arm stretching west is the original exit from the loch down the River Awe, now blocked by a dam, in a narrow and gloomy defile. It is interesting to paddle around the small islands and crannogs on the west side of the loch near the Ardanaiseig Hotel and gardens. The village of Inistrynich lies on the east side. A few kilometres further down there is a jetty and pier on the west shore, and the Ardbracknish estate to the east. The estate is not very friendly to visitors.

After a power line crossing, North Port is on the right side, at the end of a road, with the small hamlets of Annat and Kilchrenan situated a little back from the water. Portsonachan and South Port (a few houses where there used to be a small ferry) lies on the left. Although the B840 road follows the left (east) bank, it is barely visible; the right bank becomes much more wooded.

It is another 9km down the loch to the widening of Kames Bay, the entrance of the River Avich, and Dalavich are on the right bank. A forestry village is the only centre of population.

Just after this, on the left side, are two little gems, Innis Chonnell Castle (surprisingly intact)

on its island, and the larger island of Innis Sea-ramhach. The latter has an ancient burial ground; it is easy to land and walk around.

The southern end of the loch is very wooded and the right side rises quite high making landing awkward. Right at the end, the loch seems to disappear, but it has in fact turned a sharp bend to the right into a sheltered bay, the harbour and moorings for Ford village.

Variation

Loch Avich is worth a visit, a small piece of water on the west side, higher up than Loch Awe. The loch is 5km long and accessed from the minor road which runs along the north side from Loch Awe to Kilmelford. There is a car park (913 138) near a ruined castle on an island only a few metres off the mainland. The burn coming in at the top can be paddled up for a couple of hundred metres. At the lower end is the exit of the River Avich.

The Forestry Commission and leisure

The forests covering much of Scotland were planted between the two world wars and immediately after World War II, initially to supply pit props for the coal mines, and then for building materials for new houses.

Unfortunately, as Scotland's forestry came to maturity sixty years later, the market for British timber had crashed, our timber needs being met from other countries with lower costs, especially Russia. The Commission, in possession of large tracts of land but with few ways of deriving income, found itself under mounting pressure from UK governments to justify its existence.

This has led to more environmentally-friendly new planting, to lessen the visual impact of conifer forests, and an increase in the use of forests for tourism. The most radical development has been the introduction of mountain biking, in the Scottish Borders, and in Lochaber around Fort William. More recently, the use of lochs and forests for canoe and kayak touring has been recognised.

© Crannog near Dalavich, Loch Awe | Dave Walsh

© Loch Voil, Balquhidder | Dave Walsh

16 Balquhidder

 OS Sheet 57 | **River Larig, Loch Doine, Loch Voil, River Balvaig, Loch Luibnaig** | **21.5km**

Shuttle   12 miles, 30 minutes, via Balquhidder minor road, and A84.

Start   △ River Larig (453 186).

Finish   ○ Loch Lubnaig car park (585 107).

Introduction

The Balquhidder area is beautiful. Few other places in Scotland offer both lochs and an easy river. The distance is not too great and there are no awkward portages or demanding terrain. A campsite is situated about a day's journey from the start. It makes an ideal weekend trip and is suitable for beginners.

Loch Voil is peaceful once you are out and away from the road, and Loch Lubnaig has a backdrop of Ben Ledi to the west. Loch Lomond and Trossachs National Park has in recent years spent much time and money 'cleaning up' sites in the five eastern lochs (Earn, Voil, Lubnaig, Venacher, Achray) for which they are responsible. The mess was caused by irresponsible camping.

The parking where the River Balvaig leaves Loch Voil has ben expanded and improved and the two main sites on Loch Lubnaig have been transformed. The car parks are pay and display, with picnic and camping facilities. The Forestry Commission site in Strathyre has also been improved.

Description

Access the River Larig near the top of the glen. The road comes near to the river about half a kilometre before a car park. Boats can be off-loaded quickly in a passing place. The river is slow and just wide enough for open canoes. After 1.5 km, it flows into Loch Doine (no road access), and after another 1.5 km, a tiny river of 200m or so connects this top loch with the 6km long Loch Voil.

The left side of Loch Voil has the road all the way along it, whilst the right (south) side is much quieter for stops. Where the river joins Loch Voil, the brightly-painted summerhouse on the right bank is used by contemplating Buddhists visiting the centre further down Loch Voil.

Approaching the end of Loch Voil and Balquhidder village, the River Balvaig leaves on the right-hand side, and flows under the old stone road bridge, with parking on the left side of the bridge. The river then winds in long bends and you will face in every direction on the trip downriver. There is time to appreciate the geography of the surrounding hills! There are small rapids for the first kilometre or so, with possible wading in dry periods. The river then slows down, and Strathyre village is 6.5km downstream, on the A84 from Callander to Crianlarich.

About halfway down, a minor road (which also runs down to Strathyre), comes close on the right side of the river. A cable for a tiny ferry crosses the river here (it is used to carry sheep across - be assured, they don't do this unsupervised!).

Strathyre village appears quite suddenly after a stretch between trees, and an old ford or weir. The village is just to the left of the bridge and has pubs, restaurants, and a shop. Parking is difficult on the bridge approaches. Two small rapids follow after the bridge, and there is a Forestry Commission car park on the left bank where a footbridge crosses the river. It is signposted from Strathyre village, and there is a café at the entrance. The campsite is about 200m downstream of the bridge on the left side. It is about a kilometre from the campsite down to Loch Lubnaig.

Loch Lubnaig is one of the area's scenic delights … a very highland-looking loch amongst green mountains. There is a main road on the east side which can be busy. The west side has forestry cabins and is a bit more private and quiet.

As the Balvaig enters the loch, down a straight reed-lined channel, there is a parking place on the left, on the main road. There are two other car parks on the loch, both off the road, with camping and picnic facilities. They are a further 4.5 and 5.5km down the loch.

Egress is at the last car park, nearly at the end of the 6km loch. Beyond here there is a slow and reedy stretch which becomes the River Leny, often used by anglers.

Campsites

There are commercial campsites at Strathyre and camping facilities on the east shore of Loch Lubnaig.

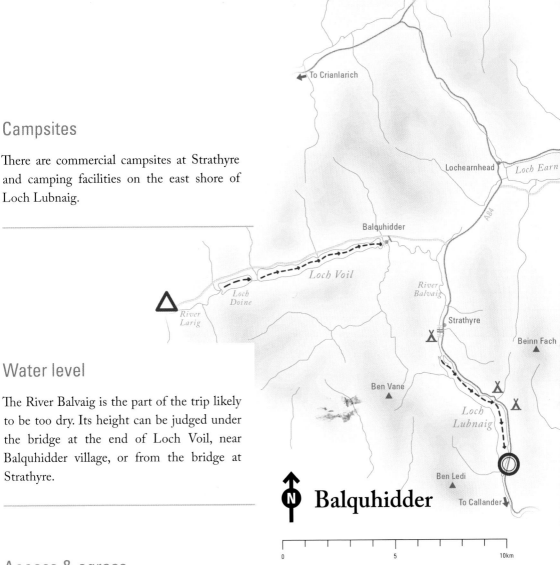

Water level

The River Balvaig is the part of the trip likely to be too dry. Its height can be judged under the bridge at the end of Loch Voil, near Balquhidder village, or from the bridge at Strathyre.

Access & egress

Although this is an enjoyable and easy trip once on the water, access by road is difficult because there is only one single-track road up this glen which can be very busy in summer. Specific parking places are referred to because of this. Loch Lubnaig is very popular as it is the nearest lochside facility to towns such as Stirling.

To avoid difficulties, you should consider keeping this route for a time outside of mid-summer and weekends. Coming here in spring or autumn and avoiding school holidays will reduce traffic issues. One of the main reasons for congestion in Balquhidder village is Rob Roy's grave.

The start is on River Larig, from a passing-place (no parking) (453 186). There is access to Loch Voil at its eastern end at a lay-by near the bridge over the River Balvaig (535 207). There is access and egress at Strathyre, at the Forestry Commission site on the left side of the river (559 168), at the campsite (559 163), at the top end of Loch Lubnaig (564 151), the first large car park on Loch Lubnaig (586 118), and the last car park (585 107).

⬜ Loch Long | ©iStockphoto.com Ewan Loughlin

The Cowal Peninsula

An Introduction

Cowal is a quiet corner of Scotland, five fingers of scenic landscape reaching out towards the Clyde, with long, sinuous sea lochs reaching deep into the heart of the area. Cloaked in heather and green forests, the peninsula is a delightful haven. Apart from an approach by sea, it can be reached by the spectacular 'Rest and Be Thankful' pass on the A83. The Ardgarten Visitor Centre is at its eastern end.

Cowal has some of the finest loch and mountain scenery in Scotland, including Loch Eck with a prehistoric freshwater herring, the 'Arrochar Alps' well-known to climbers, and the Kyles of Bute made famous in the Para Handy tales. The rock in this area is over 600 million years old, in the form of Dalriada schist. Man has laid his mark on the area since prehistory; Adam's Grave can be seen just north of Dunoon, a Neolithic burial site dating from 3,500 BC (the tomb chamber now visible as the cairn stones are missing).

This is the land of the Lamonts, Campbells and MacNaughtons. Kilmun near Dunoon has a medieval church with stone effigies of important Campbells. Cairndow, originally spelt 'Cairndhubh' (black cairn), at the head of Loch Fyne, is an ancient village with a church, inn and Big House. Little or no English was spoken in this area before the 1500s. Nearby is Dunderave Castle, the ancient home of the MacNaughton clan. Further south, Kilfinan was a prehistoric druid dwelling, and has an old church, worth seeing, which was visited by St Finian.

Little remains now of Dunoon's 12th century castle in the grounds of Castle House. In 1472 King James III made Sir Colin Campbell, Earl of Argyll, Keeper of the Castle. The castle fell into disrepair when Inveraray Castle, across Loch Fyne, became the preferred residence of the Argyll family. Mary Queen of Scots is said to have stayed there. She also stayed north of Dunoon at Glenbranter with the important MacPhunn of Drip.

The southern half of Cowal saw much clan warfare between the Lamonts and Campbells in the 17th century. The Lamont clan take their name from the Norse 'lagman', the lawman. At Ardlamont, the most southerly point of Cowal, the Campbells massacred hundreds of Lamonts in 1646, burying them alive in pits. They then destroyed Toward Castle, two miles south of Inellan. Glendaruel at the head of Loch Ruel and Inverchaolain were other Lamont strongholds. The picturesque Clachan of Glendaruel, a pre-industrial village has a historic graveyard and interesting grave-slabs. Charcoal burners produced fuel here for gunpowder mills nearby.

On a more contemporary note the area supports sailing, canoeing, horse riding, walking and mountain biking. There are outdoor adventure centres at Ardentinny, Lochgoilhead and Benmore by Dunoon.

This section describes routes from Loch Lomond, near Glasgow, west to Cowal and then south onto Kintyre, the next finger of land.

17 Loch Lomond

 OS Sheet 56 | **River Falloch near Ardlui to Balmaha** | **28km**

Shuttle It is a slow journey around the loch, especially in the summer tourist season, about an hour and a half for 40 miles on sometimes narrow roads. From Ardlui down to Tarbet is an especially narrow and slow road.

Start △ Beinglas campsite (318 187).

Finish ○ Balmaha pier (416 908).

Introduction

Loch Lomond is the largest loch in Scotland, at 36km long and 6km wide at the widest point, it is one of the most useful and attractive stretches of fresh water in Britain. With its many islands, a backdrop of mountains and tourist attractions nearby, it is a favourite with canoeists and kayakers. The area is easy to reach from Glasgow. The loch is a mecca for holidaymakers and day trippers. It is a large shared resource and a very valuable asset to the area. It is perfectly possible to spend a week here, discovering many hidden places by canoe every day. This stretch of water also offers other watersports such as sailing. Motorised water craft also use the loch and are most noticeable at weekends. There is plenty of scope for walking along the banks and on the hills and mountains nearby. The West Highland Way follows the east bank.

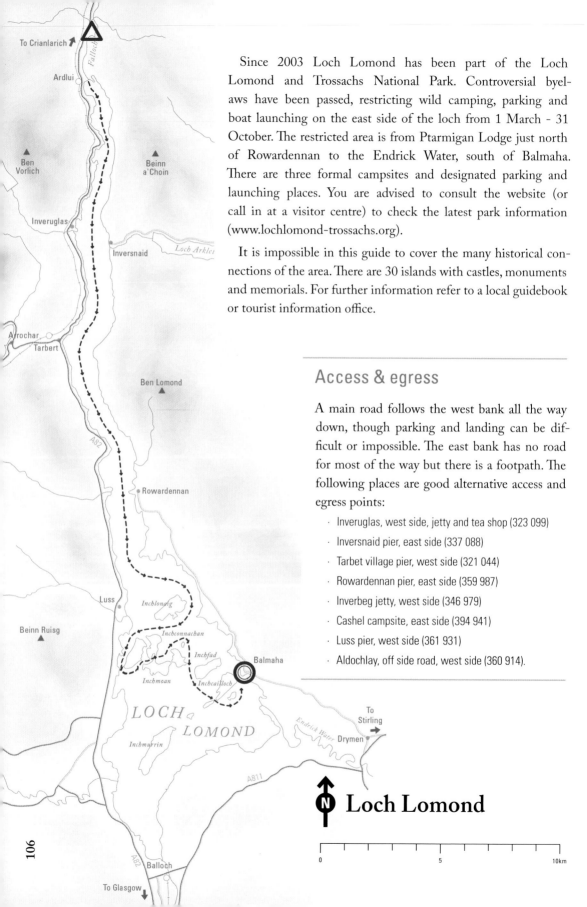

Since 2003 Loch Lomond has been part of the Loch Lomond and Trossachs National Park. Controversial byelaws have been passed, restricting wild camping, parking and boat launching on the east side of the loch from 1 March - 31 October. The restricted area is from Ptarmigan Lodge just north of Rowardennan to the Endrick Water, south of Balmaha. There are three formal campsites and designated parking and launching places. You are advised to consult the website (or call in at a visitor centre) to check the latest park information (www.lochlomond-trossachs.org).

It is impossible in this guide to cover the many historical connections of the area. There are 30 islands with castles, monuments and memorials. For further information refer to a local guidebook or tourist information office.

Access & egress

A main road follows the west bank all the way down, though parking and landing can be difficult or impossible. The east bank has no road for most of the way but there is a footpath. The following places are good alternative access and egress points:

- Inveruglas, west side, jetty and tea shop (323 099)
- Inversnaid pier, east side (337 088)
- Tarbet village pier, west side (321 044)
- Rowardennan pier, east side (359 987)
- Inverbeg jetty, west side (346 979)
- Cashel campsite, east side (394 941)
- Luss pier, west side (361 931)
- Aldochlay, off side road, west side (360 914).

Loch Lomond

0   5   10km

Campsites

There are many formal campsites in the area (there is a lovely new one at Sallochy on the east bank). Be careful when wild camping, and follow park rules.

Plans to further restrict camping on the islands and waterside sites around the park were shelved as a result of a very active campaign. However they still remain a potential threat.

Description

Loch Lomond is large, very large! In calm weather the place is a delight, but the nearness of the west coast means that strong winds blow fairly frequently. They are usually from the south-west and because of the fetch big waves can build rapidly. The weather can change very quickly, cloud over Ben Lomond on the east side can turn to rain in minutes. Trips should be planned with these factors in mind, safety being uppermost, and 'escape routes' thought about in advance.

The start is at Beinglas campsite (318 187), which is 3 kilometres north of Loch Lomond, and reached by crossing the River Falloch via a bridge off the main road. The river is slow moving and easy down to the loch.

The A82 road follows the west bank. The first part of the loch is narrow, with a 'hemmed-in' feeling compared to the southern end. It is always quieter however, and some paddlers prefer to stay at this end. About 3km down is I Vow Island with a castle, and a bit further on is Rob Roy's Cave on the left bank. Inveruglas Isle and Castle follow on the right side, then Wallace's Isle and a caravan site. High up on the right side the pipes leading down from the Loch Sloy dam to the hydroelectric power station on the loch are visible. After 7.5km Inversnaid pier and hotel are on the left, a minor road leads to the Trossach lochs further east.

After 11km the first main settlement on the right bank is Tarbet, with a 3km portage west to Loch Long. Tarbet is always busy in the summer. There are hotels, shops and a pier frequently used by pleasure boats.

The next area of interest and activity is 7km further on, with Rowardennan on the left, and Inverbeg on the right. A ferry runs between them in summer. Rowardennan is well known in canoeing circles, as the former site of the Scottish Sprint Kayak Championships. It has a thriving youth hostel just north of the village, and the hotel is in a useful position just off the water. A large car park marks the start of the Ben Lomond footpath.

The next 7km mark a narrowing of the loch followed by the Ross Isles on the left, worth landing on. Loch Lomond then widens out, with a large expanse of water before Inchlonaig (all of the islands are the Scottish 'Inch' something). On the left, a distance of some 28km from the start, is Cashel campsite which is very popular because it has good access to the water with a shingle beach.

Behind Inchlonaig to the west is Luss village with all the usual amenities, a very large car park and a sandy beach, packed in the summer. From this part of the loch circular trips can be made of the islands. When deciding which way around to go, consider the wind direction, as the islands provide useful shelter. All the islands are wooded, some have sandy beaches and others are rocky. It is often only a kilometre or two from one island to the other, and an intrepid-feeling trip can be made, even when the weather appears daunting.

Luss with its near neighbours of Inchtavannach and Inchconnachan to the south, provide a good haunt for canoeists with a delightful narrow passage between the islands. Inchconnachan is famous for its population of wallabies who seem to live quite happily there. These islands lie off Aldochlay which is on a minor road off the main west bank road, where there is a landing and some parking. Bandry Bay to the south has an interesting statue in the middle of it. To the east is Inchmoan with sandy beaches to lie on and Inchgalbraith Castle just off it.

Paddling further east are The Geggles, a very narrow passage which has caught out many a power boat, then Inchcrum and the small Buccinch. Inchfad is to the south-east and has a crannog, Ellanderroch, off its south-west shore. It is a short hop over to Inchcailloch, a nature reserve that is wardened, only some 200m off Balmaha. The east bank at this point, offers campsites at Sallochy, Cashel, and Milarrochy. The Loch Lomond Sailing Club's boathouse which houses many sailing canoes is here.

Our trip ends at Balmaha, avoiding the crowded and windswept southern end of the loch. The village has a marina, shops, cafés, and hotels and is 33km from the top of the loch. On a day when the wind puts the paddler off going anywhere, it is possible to set off from Balmaha and cross to Inchcailloch for a walk around. A path leads to the highest point on the island, with great views of the whole loch.

© Loch Eck, Cowal | Eddie Palmer

18 Loch Eck to Lochgoilhead

 OS Sheets 56 & 63 | **Loch Eck, River Eachaig, Loch Long & Loch Goil** | **44km**

Shuttle   Via the A81 to Strachur, A815 north, and then B839 (narrow and twisting) over to Lochgoilhead, 15 miles, about 30-40 minutes.

Start   △ At Glenbranter on River Cur, above Loch Eck (115 978).

Finish   ○ Lochgoilhead (191 010).

Introduction

An interesting and varied trip encompassing, unusually, a large inland loch, a short river and a coastal strip where the usual care is required. Dunoon, the major centre for Cowal, is only just off the route and has shops and facilities.

There are two recommended ways to undertake this journey. The first is to paddle down Loch Eck, camp overnight and then catch the tide the next day, setting off at half ebb tide for Holy Loch to get the full flood tide for most of Loch Long and Loch Goil. The other is to use the ebb tide down Holy Loch and then fight the ebb up to Gairletter Point where the night is spent. Use the flood the next day for the rest of the trip. The tides are not too strong. HW in the area is around the same time as HW Greenock.

Loch Eck is long and narrow with high mountains on the west side. It is very quiet, though popular with anglers. The open sea lochs give views of the whole upper Clyde, which is urban and busy, followed by the quiet and wooded Loch Goil.

The coastal part of the trip requires care, although there are only 9km of coast without a public road between Ardentinny and Carrick Castle.

Be aware that shipping is banned from the east side of Loch Long due to the defence installations. The actual area of the restricted zone is detailed on Admiralty charts and MOD boats may stop you. Keep close to the west shore.

Water level

The River Eachaig can be very low in summer, requiring a portage down to Holy Loch. Holy Loch should preferably be paddled at high tide.

Campsites

There are campsites at Invereck, south of Loch Eck, at Lochgoilhead, and Gairletter Point, and south of Ardentinny on Loch Long.

Description

The best place to launch is about a mile before Loch Eck, where the River Cur comes close to the road and there is a clearing and bridge over into an area of forest walks. Just downstream is a spot where the Cur is not too shallow and vehicles can be parked. Although the main road follows Loch Eck along the whole of its length, apart from a couple of picnic places with parking, there

© *Lochgoilhead | Eddie Palmer*

Loch Eck to Lochgoilhead

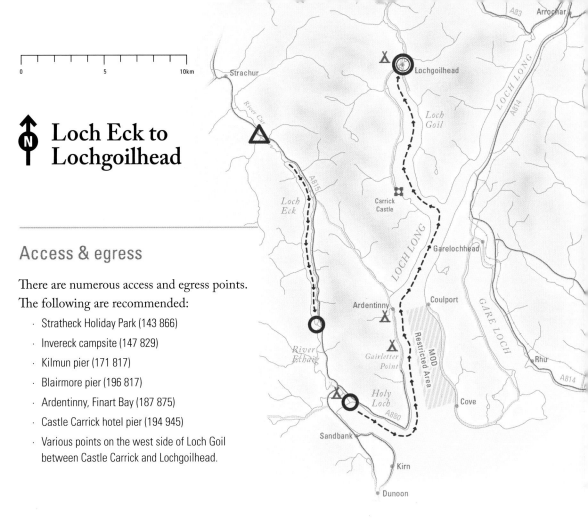

Access & egress

There are numerous access and egress points.
The following are recommended:

- Stratheck Holiday Park (143 866)
- Invereck campsite (147 829)
- Kilmun pier (171 817)
- Blairmore pier (196 817)
- Ardentinny, Finart Bay (187 875)
- Castle Carrick hotel pier (194 945)
- Various points on the west side of Loch Goil between Castle Carrick and Lochgoilhead.

are few parking places on the road. The loch can, as with all long lochs, be subject to winds from the south-east. The scenery is very Scottish and fjord-like, with mixed woodland. At the end is Stratheck Holiday Park, a large caravan site but with no camping.

Take care on the River Eachaig, 5km of delight. The start is fast and stony with several tight bends, in places large rocks create interesting little rapids. Near the Benmore Botanic Gardens the water flows fast under a footbridge then a roadbridge, followed by a very pretty narrow wooded section. Halfway down, a minor road runs alongside on the right bank. The river then winds quietly around the campsite at Invereck.

The river becomes tidal at the main road junction where the A880 leaves the Dunoon road for the side of Holy Loch. The scenery suddenly becomes maritime and much more built up. The road hugs the shore to Strone Point, which is quite tame, with a few rocks off the point. From this position, it is quite a shock to realise that the large mass to the east is Glasgow! There could not be a greater contrast between the very rural scenery so far and the city nearby. The route then proceeds up to Ardentinny. Loch Long is then fairly sheltered, especially from westerlies.

The first part of Loch Long has roads both sides, but these finish at Ardentinny on the west side, and Coulport on the east after 6km.

After another 5km, Loch Goil opens out to the north-west, a gem for touring. This is a very attractive and wooded 8km loch. The head of the loch at Lochgoilhead is a good base, with a large campsite and holiday park.

19 Loch Riddon to Loch Striven

	OS Sheet 63	Loch Riddon, Kyles of Bute & Loch Striven	25km
Shuttle	7km via A886 and B836, 10 minutes.		
Start	△ Near Ardachuple Farm, Loch Riddon (012 793).		
Finish	◎ Craigendive on Loch Striven (051 836).		

Introduction

This route is on the outermost part of the Firth of Clyde. It is suitable for canoes and kayaks as it is sheltered by Bute. It is quiet, and the road alongside Loch Riddon is only busy when the ferry comes in from Bute to Colintraive. Loch Striven is a long finger of a loch with no road along most of its west side, though the road out to the exposed Strone Point makes this a relatively safe trip. (Note that the previous trip also has a Strone Point). Take the last of the ebb to exit Loch Riddon, the flood will be with you up Loch Striven. At mid-tide, spring tides run fast around the Burnt Islands.

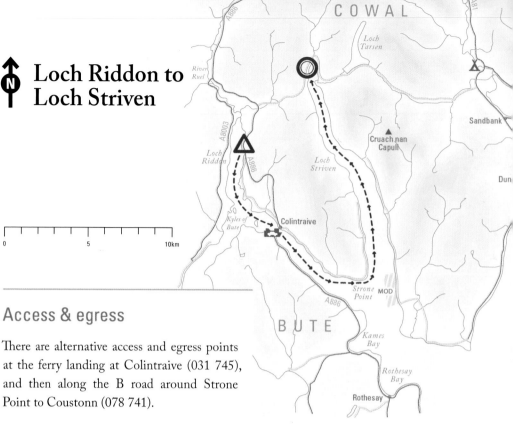

Loch Riddon to Loch Striven

Access & egress

There are alternative access and egress points at the ferry landing at Colintraive (031 745), and then along the B road around Strone Point to Coustonn (078 741).

Campsites

The only formal site in the immediate area is Glendaruel, north of Loch Riddon. Invereck, near Dunoon is the next nearest.

Description

Loch Riddon lies to the north of Bute. It is 5km long, and the northern half dries out at low tide. Access the start by parking in a lay-by on the main A886 road, by the entrance to Ardachuple Farm, and carry the boats down to the lochside over the entrance road. The loch is quiet with moored boats and a very wooded and rocky shoreline. The B866, which is very winding, follows the loch on the left side. The kyle is interesting with islands and shallows, Bute is on the right, and there is a buoyed channel between the islands. Watch out for the ferries crossing from Bute to Colintraive. The area is very wooded and the scenery pleasant. The road on the mainland side should not be used for parking as it provides access to private houses and is very narrow, with passing places only.

Near Strone Point the view opens out and the MOD submarine refuelling depot at Ardyne Point comes into sight. Further up the loch there is a tanker jetty. This area is patrolled and access is restricted on the east side, so hug the west shore when turning up Loch Striven.

Loch Striven is 13km long, a narrow isolated loch with no road up the west side. Landing is at the top of the loch on the west side where the road joins the lochside.

HW in the area is around 15- 20 minutes before HW Greenock.

Isle of Bute

It would be a great pity to have come so far and not visit Bute itself, often described as the most accessible of the west coast islands, an 'emerald gem with golden beaches set in a sea of azure blue'.

The countryside is craggy, heather-covered moorlands in the north of the island and gently rolling hills in the centre. The southern end is dominated by the busy Firth of Clyde and the fleshpots of Rothesay, which is undergoing a revival as a seaside resort, having been left behind by the overseas tourist boom since the 1960s.

Shipping regularly passes up the channel between Bute and the Cumbraes, ferries go in and out of Ardrossan to the south and Rothesay itself, and the busy marina at Largs is just to the east behind Great Cumbrae.

The island is well known for walking, cycling and cottage holidays, and outside of Rothesay is pastoral and quiet.

Bute was settled at least 2,000 years ago and has standing stones at Ettrick Bay, a vitrified Iron Age fort at Dunagoil and the ancient chapel of St Blane.

The island has one of the Victorian age's great Scottish sights, Mount Stuart, the Gothic palace of the Marquess of Bute. The mansion has a stunning interior with many fine works of art and treasures. The house, which has recently been opened to the public, has

wonderful gardens, Bute being set in a very sheltered position on the Clyde. The former racing driver, Johnny Dunbar, is one of the family.

Rothesay, with its Victorian frontage overlooking the bay, is connected to Glasgow during the summer by the steamer 'Waverley'. Ardencraig Gardens, near Rothesay, have beautiful floral displays in the summer and an exotic bird aviary.

Scalpsie Bay on the west coast, overlooking Arran, has a large colony of seals and Inchmarnock is a small island set almost at the crossroads between Bute, Arran and Kintyre. The narrowing channel which heads north is the West Kyle of Bute, leading to the attractive village of Tighnabruich, a major sailing centre. The area is used for teaching and training would-be sailors, as it considered very safe.

The West Kyle is protected by the most westerly Cowal peninsula, ending at Ardlamont Point. On the west side of this finger of land is Portvadie, an impossibly small port with a ferry over Loch Fyne to Tarbert on Kintyre. Improbably, Portavadie was the embarkation port for a ferry service to Northern Ireland which lasted only for a couple of years.

The East Kyle is around the north end of Bute between the Burnt Isles and the narrow ferry crossing at Colintraive.

20 Tayvallich & Loch Sween

OS Sheets 62 & 65 | Tayvallich to Castle Sween | 12-34km

Shuttle	If done as a round trip, no shuttle; if a one-way day trip, a slow drive up the B8025 towards Crinan, and then down the minor road to Castle Sween, some 16 miles, 40 minutes.
Start	△ Tayvallich (740 872).
Finish	○ Castle Sween (715 790).

Introduction

This area is very useful for paddlers – further south is the coast of Kintyre with no area as sheltered for paddlers, though many trips for experienced sea kayakers. Loch Sween and its inlets have much to offer, from very wooded areas to the bare and isolated islands down the peninsula from Tayvallich. The village of Tayvallich is a yachting centre with a very sheltered harbour, and Carsaig Bay and the Sound of Jura are under a kilometre to the west.

The Crinan Canal and the village of Crinan are nearby to the north, and just further north still is Kilmartin Glen, one of the most interesting prehistoric sites of Scotland with many signs of ancient habitation. The route described is down the loch to Castle Sween, it is straightforward, especially in calm weather.

Description

The head of Loch Sween has three inlets which may be explored. Caol Scotnish has a heronry in the forest, and woodland birds visit the rocks in the tidal area. Around the corner on the western side of the main loch are the Fairy Islands, a peaceful area of lagoons, sandbars and wooded islands. Strone is at the head of the loch. The eastern arm has a long head which dries out and the island of Eilean Loain which can be paddled around.

About two-thirds of the way down Loch Sween is Castle Sween, with a campsite and grocery shop. In the summer many boats are moored here, and speed boats with water skiers are sometimes encountered.

On the opposite, west side there is a large hidden inlet, Linne Mhuirich, behind Taynish Island and the Ulva Islands. A canoe can navigate through the narrow passages and shallow water. Further south is the Island of Danna, a possible circumnavigation in calm conditions.

Access & egress

There are few obvious alternative points, due to rugged sides of the loch, but emergency landings could be made at various places.

Campsites

There are sites at Tayvallich and Castle Sween.

Tayvallich & Loch Sween

Caol Scotnish | Judy Unkles

The Crinan Canal

This short waterway does not merit a route of its own. It is nevertheless an engineering marvel, and to visit Tayvallich and not see something of the canal would be a missed opportunity. The Crinan was designed to cut through the narrowest neck of land in Kintyre, avoiding the dangerous voyage around the Mull of Kintyre, and it is still an attraction for yachtsmen who want to save a couple of days travel.

Construction began in 1794 and it opened in 1801. Poor engineering meant that the water was never at the correct level, and locks and reservoirs collapsed. Thomas Telford redesigned it in 1816 and the locks were reconstructed and deepened in the 1930s.

It is only 9 miles from Ardrishaig on Loch Fyne to Crinan on the Sound of Jura, but with 15 locks and restrictions, it will normally take a large boat 6 hours to traverse.

The highest point on the canal is 65 feet above sea level. Seven reservoirs feed the canal to ensure the locks do not dry out (a wonderful engineering calculation). The locks drain down into the flat land to the north of the canal.

From the eastern end the Crinan winds its way around the back of the town of Ardrishaig. It follows the A83 road northwards up to Lochgilphead (the loch here dries out at every tide). There is a long stretch without locks and then after Lochgilphead the canal turns westward to Cairnbaan, with a flight of locks, a hotel and restaurants.

© Looking south over Tayvallich Bay | Judy Unkles

More locks at Dunardy mark the highest stretch (less than a mile long) – no rest for crews who then start downhill again. Bellanoch has a marina amongst the trees on the south side, and Loch Crinan is to the right. After a narrow stretch cut through rock, the village of Crinan; with its large basin, harbour and hotel is a picturesque spot.

Variation

The McCormaig Islands are 1km from the mouth of Loch Sween. They can be reached in calm weather, though care should be taken as even expert sea kayakers have failed to reach the islands despite several attempts.

Eilean Mor, the largest of the four McCormaigs, is worth a visit. At one point this was a 'motorway' stop for the sea traffic between Ireland and Scotland, so it is not surprising that a passing saint stayed to become a hermit. The cave, chapel and cross can all still be seen.

Perthshire & Stirlingshire

An Introduction

This area is one of the most diverse and historic in Scotland, with lochs and forests to the north, and Loch Lomond and Trossachs National Park to the west. Two large river systems drain the catchments, the Tay and Forth. To the southeast is Loch Leven, famous for its historical association with Mary, Queen of Scots, and also a National Nature Reserve due to abundant wintering geese. At the RSPB reserve here you may see ducks, whooper swans, redshanks, and lapwings as well as pink-footed geese. There is also access for water-users during the summer.

North of the Roman Antonine Wall, between Edinburgh and Glasgow, a line of Roman signal stations stretched from near Stirling up to Perth, on an escarpment north of the Allan Water and the lower reaches of the River Earn.

The Stirling area has many connections with the Scottish Wars of Independence, with four battle sites in the Stirling-Falkirk area, and many castles to visit. One of the most famous was the Battle of Stirling Bridge, where William Wallace and Andrew Moray defeated the English under Edward I in 1297. The Scots, descending from the heights where the Wallace Monument now stands, caught the heavily-armoured English on the narrow bridge over the Forth, and the boggy ground where Causewayhead now stands. The former bridge is somewhere between the modern road bridge and the medieval one which is now a footbridge. Stirling Castle is one of the largest and best-preserved, ranking alongside Edinburgh Castle; it is very visible above the city on its high rock. The Wallace Monument is also prominent to the north east.

In 1298, Wallace was routed at the Battle of Falkirk on 22nd July by Edward I, at the site which is now Victoria Park. The park has a drinking fountain which commemorates a local nobleman who died in the battle.

Just south of Stirling, the Battle of Bannockburn took place on 23rd June 1314, when Robert the Bruce defeated Edward II. The area is a suburb of Stirling, but a visitor centre displays details of the battle. A few miles to the north-west is Doune Castle, on the River Teith.

Falkirk has a regenerated water transport connection with the rest of Scotland, the Falkirk Wheel canal lift is a modern wonder of the world, and the largest of its kind, lifting water traffic from the Forth and Clyde Canal into the Union Canal.

Far to the north, at Killiecrankie in Perthshire, during the first Jacobite uprising, government troops were attacked in 1689 in the beautiful wooded gorge by the side of the River Garry. The Jacobite forces were led by John Graham of Claverhouse, 'Bonny Dundee', and he was killed in the action. Losses on both sides were heavy, the Highlanders were unable to capitalise on their success, and were defeated at Dunkeld, on the River Tay, three weeks later. The 'Soldier's Leap', across a narrows on the Garry, commemorates the place where it is said an English soldier escaped the Jacobites by jumping across the river.

The Tay catchment is one of the largest, if not the largest, in Scotland. The other two rivers, the Earn and Teith, are perhaps less well known.

© Kenmore and Loch Tay | VisitScotland/ScottishViewpoint

21 The Tay System

 OS Sheets 50, 51, 52 & 53 | Crhianlarich to Perth | 101km

Shuttle	53 miles, 1.5 hours via A85, Crieff to Perth, one way.
Portages	Corriechaorach and Lix rapids, River Dochart; Falls of Dochart just before Loch Tay; and possibly Grandtully and Stanley Weir, River Tay.
Start	△ Crianlarich (385 255).
Finish	◎ North Inch, Perth (120 240).

Introduction

No visit to Scotland would be complete without a visit to the River Tay. It carries the highest flow in Scotland, and one of the highest in the UK. The Tay drains an enormous area, which is why it stays up when all else has gone down, and the loch above is a mammoth cistern holding its water. The watercourses draining into Loch Tay rise only a few miles from the west coast. The Cononish on Ben Lui, for example, is only 12 miles from Loch Etive.

The Dochart makes a pleasant start to this trip, even with a portage around the Falls of Dochart at Killin. It's a small, attractive river with a couple of good rapids (grade 2-3). The valley is the corridor to the West Highlands, which you drive up along the A82 through Crianlarich and Tyndrum.

Loch Tay is some 24km long, from Killin to Kenmore, where the river Tay leaves. The loch is fringed by mountains, with the Ben Lawers range filling the horizon to the north. Together, the two rivers and loch provide a possible four-day trip with usually reliable water, and great scenery.

The River Tay is a Scottish classic. It flows through a wooded valley, widening to take in the River Tummel near Pitlochry, narrowing again through the 'Highland gap' at Dunkeld, before meandering through fertile farmland down to Perth. Some 75km of paddling, usually without portages or wading, and a further 40km of estuary below Perth. There are two famous grade 3 stretches of whitewater, Grandtully and Stanley, both straightforward, with easier grade 2 rapids elsewhere.

There are roads alongside both the Dochart and Tay, and the main A9 is near to the river from Pitlochry down to Perth. Vehicle shuttles are straightforward.

Access & egress

The River Dochart is accessed from the A85, at Crianlarich (385 255), with egress above the Falls of Dochart (563 318). A minor road follows the north bank down the lower stretch, useful for inspecting the Lix rapids.

Access to Loch Tay is usually from the Killin Hotel car park (573 334) onto the short River Lochay. Permission should be sought for this and vehicles parked elsewhere. The A827 follows the north side of the loch, often away from the water. There is also access at Fearnan (715 443) and at Kenmore there are several places near the watersports centre and car park (772 456).

Egress is in Perth (120 240) and there is alternative access to the River Tay at the following points:

- Aberfeldy (851 494)
- Grandtully (911 531)
- Logierait (969 519)
- Dunkeld (027 425)
- Caputh (089 394)
- Kinclaven (Bridge of Isla) (163 382)
- Stanley (119 338)
- Luncarty (101 300)
- Waulkmill (106 290).

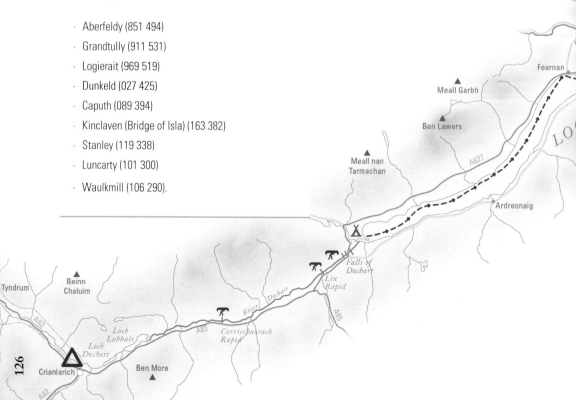

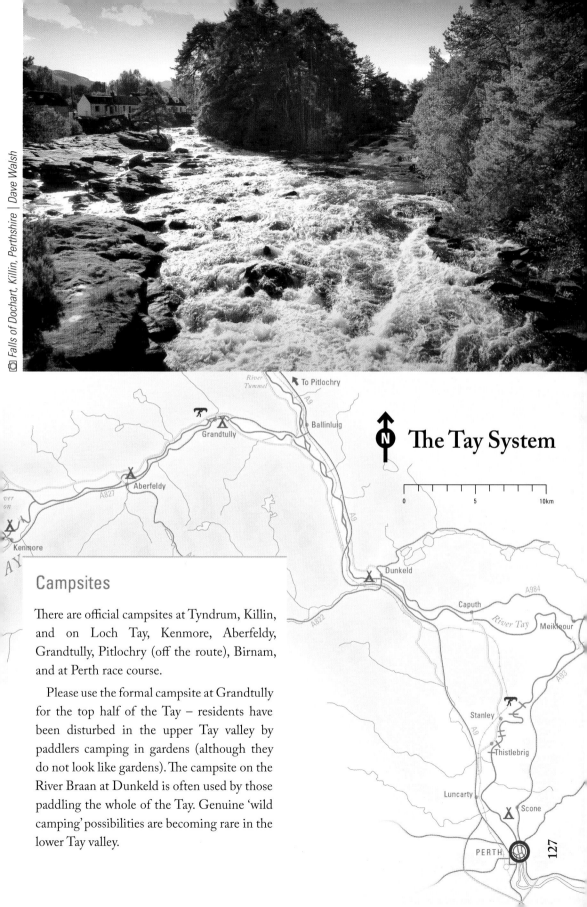

The Tay System

Campsites

There are official campsites at Tyndrum, Killin, and on Loch Tay, Kenmore, Aberfeldy, Grandtully, Pitlochry (off the route), Birnam, and at Perth race course.

Please use the formal campsite at Grandtully for the top half of the Tay – residents have been disturbed in the upper Tay valley by paddlers camping in gardens (although they do not look like gardens). The campsite on the River Braan at Dunkeld is often used by those paddling the whole of the Tay. Genuine 'wild camping' possibilities are becoming rare in the lower Tay valley.

Water level

The Dochart is a small river. At the Lix rapids, a visual inspection should be made to check whether they can be paddled.

Loch Tay is a large body of water, and the River Tay can be paddled in almost any water. For much of the year the River Tay tends to be high when other rivers have lost their water. A look at the river at Grandtully from the bank gives a good idea of the water level, as does the SEPA gauge (see the SCA website).

SUGGESTED ITINERARY

Day 1 – Crianlarich to opposite Ardeonaig, Loch Tay (35km – 7 hours)

Day 2 – Loch Tay to Grandtully campsite (35km – 6 hours)

Day 3 – Grandtully to Dunkeld/Birnam (20km – 4 hours), or Caputh (29km – 5 hours)

Day 4 – Birnam to Perth (37km – 6 hours), or Caputh to Perth (28km – 5 hours)

Description

The valley at Crianlarich is fairly flat-bottomed, and the Dochart, having tumbled down a narrow valley, is now as flat as a canal. It is 22km from here to Killin. Crianlarich railway bridge, over the A85, is the key to access; just downstream of the railway bridge, from the north side of the A85, there is a grass track leading down to the south bank of the river. Camping is not allowed.

© Wade's Bridge, Aberfeldy, River Tay | Dave Walsh

There is parking on the main road in the village, and there is a store, post office, and railway station nearby.

The river flows into Loch Dochart, where there is a ruined castle on an island, and then into Loch Iubhair, which is wooded and pretty. A little exploration finds the exit where the water starts to move. The river is overhung with trees in summer, and features gentle rapids. After 10km comes the first rapid of note, Corriechaorach, which starts on the left, and moves over to the centre. It is straightforward in a kayak, and shootable in an open canoe … with care. After 14.5km and Auchlyne road bridge, the river slows down and meanders over a flat plain, with a B road on the left bank, as far as the Lix rapids. After 20km, woodland appears on the right bank, warning of rapids ahead. The Lix rapids start where the left bank becomes wooded, and the road is right alongside. The Lix Toll junction is on the A82, 1km away on the right bank.

These rapids are great for beginners as the two main drops are straightforward, followed by a rocky stretch over some 500m. The road runs right alongside. The bottom of the rapids is a good place to take out and there is lay-by on the B road (unless you also intend to run the Falls of Dochart!). From here it is 1km into Killin village, where there are hotels, tea-rooms, and shops. A good spot to rest before taking on Loch Tay.

The loch itself is worthy of a two day camping trip. The scenery is fine, and very different from the view from the road along the north side. A short day's paddle (or the afternoon if you did the Dochart in the morning) would bring you to the woodland, and waterfall 19km along the north shore, opposite Ardreonaig on the south shore where there is an outdoor centre. Camping

© The Firth of Tay from Kinnoull Hill, Perth | Dave Walsh

is possible here. Along most of the loch the roads and houses are not very visible. The road on the north side comes down to the shore near Fearnan after 18km (another outdoor centre here).

Kenmore has a castle, two crannogs, a watersports centre, car parking, two hotels, and the entrance to the Tay, with a camp and caravan site on the left.

Just under 2km after entering the Tay there is a first substantial rapid, known as Chinese Bridge. The line is straight down, but if in doubt, when you see the bridge, land on the right bank and inspect. The waves are large and can swamp an open canoe.

Further down there is a good flow of water, small shingle rapids, islands, and the River Lyon which joins from the left. Some 10km downstream lies Aberfeldy, self-styled 'Capital of Heartland Perthshire', with a whole cluster of rafting and outdoor adventure companies. Aberfeldy has good landing on the right bank, just before the very individual Wade's Bridge (named after General Wade of military and road-building fame).

About 5km further down the water speeds up and the SCA Edradynate access point marks the start of the whitewater racecourse. These rapids are big and bouncy though still grade 2 with no route-finding difficulties. If a stranger to the Tay, it is worth visiting the Grandtully site beforehand, with its car park, café and slalom site in order to recognise the approach to the rapids from the river.

After shallows, formed by an old weir, there is a bend to the left and a view of both the slalom poles and the road bridge below. The first drop comes up fast, so if you want to inspect it, land on the left bank on gabions filled with stones. Do not land on the right bank – it is too far away to inspect the drop. If wishing to land and portage, proceed over to the right bank and land amongst trees just above the first substantial rapid. Do not land in the garden of the house, or go down the old mill lade (Scots for a watercourse, especially one that carries water to a mill) on the right.

The river slows down after Grandtully, and meanders through Logierait. The River Tummel joins from the left, and the A9 is very visible on the left bank. Dunkeld comes up next, a small historic town with a cathedral.

Camping can be found, either at Birnam on the right bank, 500m or so below Dunkeld bridge (in an open area behind houses), or further on after Caputh bridge, on the right bank in the woodland.

After Caputh, the river meanders through interesting gravel banks, a mecca for water birds as this stretch is well away from roads or paths.

The next bridge, the last one before Perth, is Kinclaven. Access is awkward near the Isla bridge, as there is no right of way for vehicles. It is possible to park at the Meikleour beech hedge (a popular tourist site) on the main A93 road, pass canoes over the fence on the corner of the Kinclaven Bridge road, and walk down to the river at Isla Bridge. The beech hedge, planted in 1745, is said to be the highest in the world.

The next few kilometres are pleasant, easy but fast water, until the sudden appearance of islands signals the top of the infamous Campsie Linn (grade 3), a shock of a rapid so far down a large river. There are four shoots, with rocky and vegetated islands in between. The easiest in normal water is the second from the right, a straightforward drop. In very high water, the extreme right through trees is possible. The brave might want to shoot the left route. Campsie Linn can be portaged on the right bank.

Then in quick succession: Stanley Weir, the middle shoot is the usual one to take, then below, a series of rapids, Catspaws and Hellhole, grade 2-3, leading down to a bend to the right. After a large rapid with big waves on the right-hand bend, a flat section, and then old weirs, with the large fully restored building of Stanley Mills visible on the right bank. A fast current now winds down between harmless lines of rocks. After a pause for breath, and a bend to the left with houses built perilously high up on a crumbling sandstone cliff on the right bank is Thistlebrig Rapid (grade 3). The main flow goes from centre to left, and the white leaping waves at the end are clearly visible up-river. In high water, it is simple to go down on the right – the main tail has large waves and boils.

For those wishing to avoid grade 2-3 rapids the above section can be portaged as follows: Stanley Weir can be portaged on the left. The next half mile or so has a path down the left side. To avoid Hellhole, cross the river above it from left to right, and then portage the bend on the right. After this right-hand bend, the river is easier, but can be avoided by paddling down the mill lade on the left side, entered above the small weir, on the extreme left. The lade can be followed right down to below Thistlebrig rapid, entering the river again before the lade bends well away from the river.

From here it is a straightforward paddle down to Perth, with a choice of egress points on both banks. The usual finish is on the North Inch at Perth, a large grassy area above the first road bridge. Beyond this point the river becomes tidal and enters Perth's commercial shipping docks.

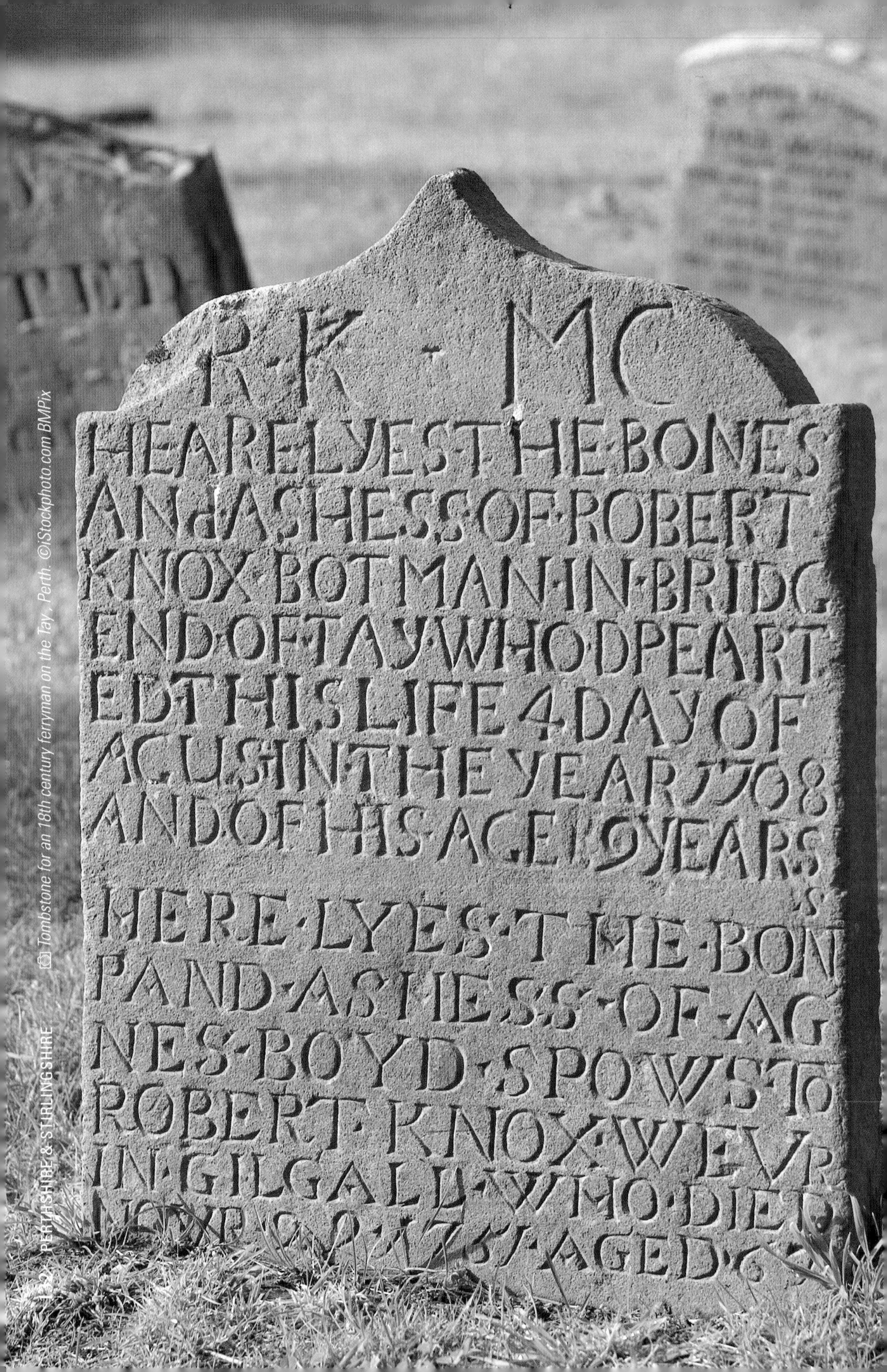

R·K · MC

HEARELYESTHEBONES
ANDASHESSOFROBERT
KNOXBOTMANINBRIDG
ENDOFTAYWHODPEART
EDTHISLIFE4DAYOF
AGUSINTHEYEAR1708
ANDOFHISAGE65YEARS

HERE·LYES·THE·BON
PAND·ASHESS·OF·AG
NES·BOYD·SPOWSTO
ROBERT·KNOX·WEVR
IN·GILGALL·WHO·DIED
NOVR·20·1737·AGED·6

22 River Earn

OS Sheets 51, 52 & 58 | **Comrie to Kinkell Bridge** | **23km**

Shuttle	16 miles, 35 minutes, via A85 and B8062.
Portages	You may choose to portage the grade 3 weirs.
Start	△ Dalchonzie power station, 1km down a minor road from a junction on the A85, 4km west of Comrie (743 225).
Finish	◎ Kinkell Bridge, signposted from both Crieff and Auchterarder (932 167).

Introduction

The Earn is a little-known river, with the potential for a long trip. The route described in this section is the most popular day's paddle. The valley runs from west to east across the south of Perthshire and the Earn flows from the mountains on the border with Stirlingshire and Highland across a wooded valley and fertile agricultural plain. The river is very small in its upper reaches when it leaves Loch Earn, one of the few Scottish lochs used by powerboats and water skiers. It grows larger below the busy village of Comrie. The next town down is Crieff, originally a spa town, which still has a large spa hotel. This stretch is pretty, with interesting features along the way. Below Crieff, although the valley flattens out and the current lessens, there are four weirs, all different, to add some spice.

Kinkell Bridge is the only river crossing for some miles, so it is well signposted. Below the bridge, the river winds for many miles arriving eventually at Bridge of Earn, its tidal limit, before joining the Tay above Newburgh.

This fairly long day trip, suitable for spring or autumn includes: a small infant river, a narrow and interesting part before Comrie, a widening out on the way down to Crieff, and a final meander across an agricultural plain down to Kinkell Bridge. The countryside is mixed agriculture, with small wooded hills.

River Earn

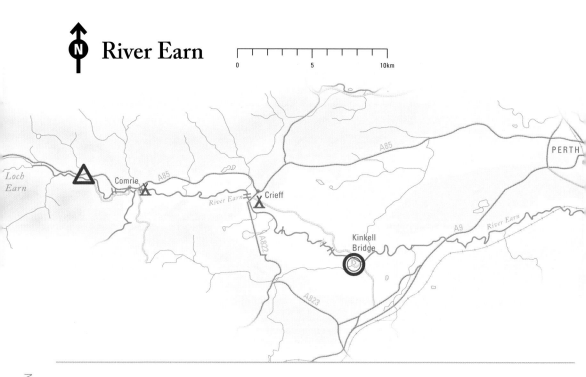

Water level

Check the level from the bridges at Comrie and Crieff.

Campsites

There is a campsite on the south side of Lochearnside, two sites at Comrie and two sites at Crieff.

Access & egress

The A85 follows the valley down from Loch Earn. The normal start is at the Dalchonzie power station (772 218). There is access and egress at Comrie (775 219), Crieff (857 209), and Kinkell Bridge (932 167).

Description

The start is at the Dalchonzie power station outflow under the minor road off the A85. The hydro-scheme is powered by water piped in from Loch Earn, 5km upstream. The river itself is seen near the A85, but often has very little water. Launch over the fence onto the outflow from the power station. The river is joined a couple of hundred yards downstream. It is small, tree-lined and pretty.

After 1.5km there is a sharp bend to the left, a fish farm on the right, and a long weir, shootable on the left side.

The excitement continues, especially for open canoe paddlers, as the river bends left down a small gorge, with a rapid, and then a weir across the left side of river. It looks like there is no room on the right, but there is a narrow passage down the right bank, with a sharp bend to the left at the bottom. The road is high up on the right bank at this point. A leafy paddle down into Comrie follows. If the water is high enough for a good trip, you will brush tree branches all the way down on this part. Comrie creeps slowly into view. At the first bridge it is hard to imagine that you are approaching a sizeable village.

At the obvious main road bridge in Comrie (5km), the town is to the left. Access is on the right bank, upstream of the bridge, via a path that goes up to convenient parking.

There is a rapid under the bridge, and then a grade 3 rocky weir, most easily portaged on the right bank. Acces is relatively easy up to a road, but parking is limited. Small rapids continue, with two larger ones nearer to Crieff.

At 9km there is sharp bend to the right, just before a very visible monument on a hill ahead. This is Laggan Hill, well-known to local residents for its long walks amongst beech woods. The river turns right, then left, under a minor road bridge.

Houses herald the start of Crieff, a large and famous spa town. It is possible to land on the right bank, just upstream from the main road bridge and, with care, egress through a caravan park and narrow walkway to a car park for the town's playing fields. The town is to the left, up a steep hill. To the right, along the main road, is a visitor centre with café and car park (open on a Sunday).

The river is broader now, with fewer rapids, but several large weirs requiring care.

Nearly 5km after Crieff is Dornoch Mill weir, which usually requires inspection, and sometimes portaging if trees are blocking the usual runs down the face. Land on the right side, away from the house on the left bank. The weir has a gradual slope, and is usually straightforward. The countryside has by now become more open, with the river winding between high banks which become increasingly wooded.

A rather long slog on slow water brings you to the ornamental Colquhalzie estate bridge, set in neat scenery. Right under the bridge is a steep weir, shootable on the extreme left. It is difficult to inspect without going ashore. The weir looks a bit fearsome, and can be exciting for open canoes, but is fairly straightforward.

You are now only a couple of kilometres from the end, but there are two further exciting bits to go; two broken weirs at Mills of Earn. The line on the first is fairly obvious, down a chute, followed 500 metres later by the second, which is quite lengthy with little wooded islands to land on.

Kinkell Bridge is now very obvious downstream. There is an egress on the left bank, just below the bridge. Take care not to disturb anglers, as the car park up the bank from here belongs to them. There is another parking area by the gate to an estate, on the bridge approaches, a few yards back along the road.

© River Teith at Callander, looking upstream to Ben Ledi | Dave Walsh

23 River Teith

OS Sheet 57 | **Callander to Stirling** | **23.5km**

Shuttle	16 miles, 30 minutes, via A84 from Callander to Stirling.
Portages	Torrie rapid may be grade 3 in high water.
	Portage the dangerous weir at Deanston.
Start	△ Callander (625 069).
Finish	◎ Stirling (796 951).

Introduction

This is an attractive small river, close to the central belt of Scotland, with the trip finishing in Stirling, just off the M9. The Teith is fed with water coming from two different directions; from the Leny, draining the rivers and lochs of Balquhidder, and from the small rivers and lochs flowing east from the Trossachs. These waterways join just as they enter Callander, an important and busy tourist town, with hotels, restaurants and other facilities. Callander is seen as the eastern gateway to the Trossachs and Loch Lomond National Park. It is attractively ringed by mountains.

The Teith is a popular beginner's whitewater river, and is an annual trip for many open boaters. The river has the quality of being interesting all the way down, with attractive scenery, and continuous small rapids. The only place likely to cause any problems in high water is Deanston weir, which can be portaged easily on the left side of the river. The river below Deanston, down to Stirling, is grade 1 to the junction with the Forth, where it becomes tidal.

Description

Callander town centre has a car park and recreation area on the left bank above the road bridge (Meadows Car Park), which is the usual launch point. The river winds slowly and prettily around the back of the town, with occasional shallows.

This first half, down to Deanston, is quite wooded and attractive. After 4km, the Keltie Water joins from the left, and there are several places with benches meant for anglers which make good picnic sites.

The approach to Torrie rapid is announced by several bends, and small slabby rapids. When a very sharp bend to the left becomes obvious, and the river disappears, you can go over to the far right side to see around the bend.

Torrie rapid is a ledge run on the extreme left. It is straightforward though the overhanging trees and rock ledge look a bit too near for comfort. After a first drop, the trick is to aim a bit to the right, away from the bank. In high water there is an enjoyable long and large wave train. There are two more small drops (formerly a slalom course) in the next 400m. At the end of the rapids

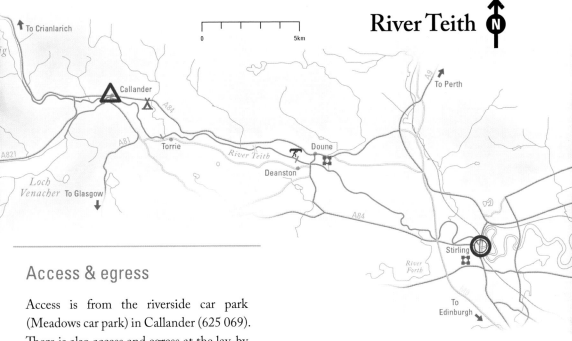

Access & egress

Access is from the riverside car park (Meadows car park) in Callander (625 069). There is also access and egress at the lay-by on the A84, near Torrie rapid (670 046), and below Deanston weir (714 016). The final egress is in Stirling on the Forth (796 951).

Campsites

There are several campsites in Callander.

Water level

The River Teith is at a nice level if it is just below the walkway in the car park in Callander. The river is visible when driving up the A84, and most rocks should be covered.

there is easy access out to the main A84 road. This is marked by a height gauge on the left bank, and there is an obvious and large lay-by, off a loop of the old road with an entrance and exit on to the main road.

The river carries on, with frequent easy rapids, and stays close to the road. About 2km further on is a country estate, with an ornate metalwork bridge, and summerhouses on the banks. There are small drops just above and below the bridge. Below here, a weir marked on the OS map has completely disappeared. The river slows down a little, an obvious horizon line heralding the weir at Deanston. The reason for the weir is the distillery which takes water off at this point.

Deanston weir is high, long, and dangerous. To portage around, look for a landing on the left bank about 200m above the weir, and scramble up a wooded bank onto a muddy track. In summer this track may be hidden by foliage. It is an easy and level walk down to below the weir where nice steps and a rope bannister lead steeply back down to the river. In very low water, it is possible to carry over the face of the weir on the extreme left.

The whole of the right side of the weir is awkward. To carry around the sluices is impossible due to a high metal gate and barbed wire, then a locked gate across the mill lade, on the way back to the riverside.

The weir can be run down the salmon steps on the right side but these should be checked for debris. The landing on the right bank is so awkward that you may choose to inspect from the left (as described for the portage). However you will be on the wrong side in terms of selecting a line and then running it.

In high water, it is possible to land on the right against the sluices, climb up, and check the salmon steps. Be warned that in very high water, the current sweeps boats against the metal grille and it is difficult to paddle back upstream.

Open canoes can be lined down the salmon steps, but the lines need to be long as there are high retaining walls running for 100m or so downstream. The steps are easier for kayaks, but they have debris in them, including metal poles and tree stumps. The face of the weir has a 1m drop at the end and a substantial stopper in high water.

After the weir, egress is possible at the water treatment works about 800m further downstream on the right, just after the wire gabions end. This point is reached by the minor road to Deanston village off the A84, turn off to the right, down to the river where the road turns sharply left.

The Teith continues to run fast down to the A84 main road bridge (from here, 7km to the junction with the River Forth). Below the bridge is Doune Castle, obvious on the left bank, and both it and the village are worth a visit.

The river now slows down, with a broken old weir, followed by several islands.

The Forth joins where both the M9 motorway and Stirling are fairly obvious up ahead. Surprisingly, the Teith often carries more water than the Forth. After 1km there is a motorway bridge, then a shallow weir, which is covered at high tide. At low tide, there are rapids below the weir, islands, a few loops of river past the entrance of Allan Water, followed by a busy road on the left bank. Egress either here, or a little further on at the old Stirling bridge (now pedestrianised), on the left side. The modern road bridge is just below, and somewhere in between there was a bridge in the 13th century, the site of the famous battle where William Wallace defeated the English army.

© Loch Ken | VisitScotland/ScottishViewpoint

Southern Gems

An Introduction

Borders region is dominated by the Tweed valley with its major river and many fast-flowing tributaries. The area is 1,800 square miles. The western part is entirely moorland and conifer forest. The land slopes gently east to rich agricultural farmland and a rocky North Sea coast. Abbeys, stately homes and museums abound.

The two itineraries described cannot do justice to the wealth and diversity of this region. Many tourists rush through to the north, either up the M74 past Dumfries and Galloway, or on the A1 near the coast, oblivious of the eastern Borders.

The history of the area is commemorated each summer by 'Ridings' through the Border towns. These horseback pageants follow the ancient boundaries of the settlements, with their origins in the necessary establishment of territory in turbulent medieval times. Near the border with England raids were carried out over the border into Northumberland, and the mayhem was reciprocated. Cattle and sheep were stolen, and the townsfolk built fortified manor houses and 'bastles' (fortified farmhouses) in defence.

In the Tweed valley you will find interesting castles and historic houses at Peebles, Melrose and Dryburgh. Further down the valley is Kelso with some unusual town centre architecture and Floors Castle. Mellerstain House is just to the north-west of Kelso, and Manderston House is to the north near Duns. The Tweed itself is festooned with ruins of castles down the length of its valley. Peebles area is enjoying a boom due to the development of the surrounding forest for mountain biking. Thousands now flock to the Forestry Commission forest trails, especially for the world-class competitions.

Dumfries and Galloway is quite different, stretching 120 miles from Gretna west to Stranraer. The rivers flow south from the high moors to the Solway Firth, however there are few rivers of any great length or volume.

The scenery is very varied, from deserted sandy beaches and lonely estuaries to rich farmland, coastal machair, wooded river valleys and the moorland of the Southern Uplands. The Ken and Dee system appears in this book because, apart from the pleasant scenery there is always a good depth of water as a result of the damming of the valley.

Historical interests are well served by Drumlanrig Castle, north of Dumfries, built between 1679 and 1691, Dundrennan Abbey at Kirkcudbright, and Glenluce Abbey in the west. Near Dalbeattie is Orchardton Tower, Palnackie, the only Scottish tower built in the cylindrical Irish style, and to the east at Lockerbie, Rammerscales House, an 18th century sandstone manor.

The area has a much milder climate than most of Scotland, enabling the cultivation of some breathtaking gardens. Threave Castle, virtually on the Dee at Castle Douglas, has magnificent gardens, as has Castle Kennedy near Stranraer.

📷 Red kites may be seen over the wooded banks of Loch Ken | ©Stockxpert.com Marilyn Barbone

Loch Ken | Sue Brighouse

24 Loch Ken & River Dee

OS Sheets 77 & 83 | St John's Town of Dalry to Bridge of Dee | 23/34km

Shuttle	Two routes: either A713, A75 and A711 via Castle Douglas, 21 miles, 40 minutes, or A762 and A711 via Tongland, 20 miles, 35 minutes.
Portages	Over the dam at Glenlochar, end of Loch Ken.
Start	△ Alangibbon bridge, St John's Town of Dalry (615 820).
Finish	◎ Bridge of Dee (734 600).

Introduction

Galloway is an unhurried and quiet area of Scotland. It offers peace and quiet and plenty of wildlife. People come here for cottage holidays, birdwatching and outdoor activities. The river and loch system offers many different types of paddling. The river sections are generally grade 2 and, together with the long and narrow Loch Ken, make a decent open canoe trip from below Allangibbon Bridge, near St John's Town of Dalry. The placid loch gives fairly safe paddling without too much wind, and is a haven for wildfowl. With a pleasant campsite halfway down, the route offers a nice and easy introduction to canoe camping with a 'getting away from it all' atmosphere.

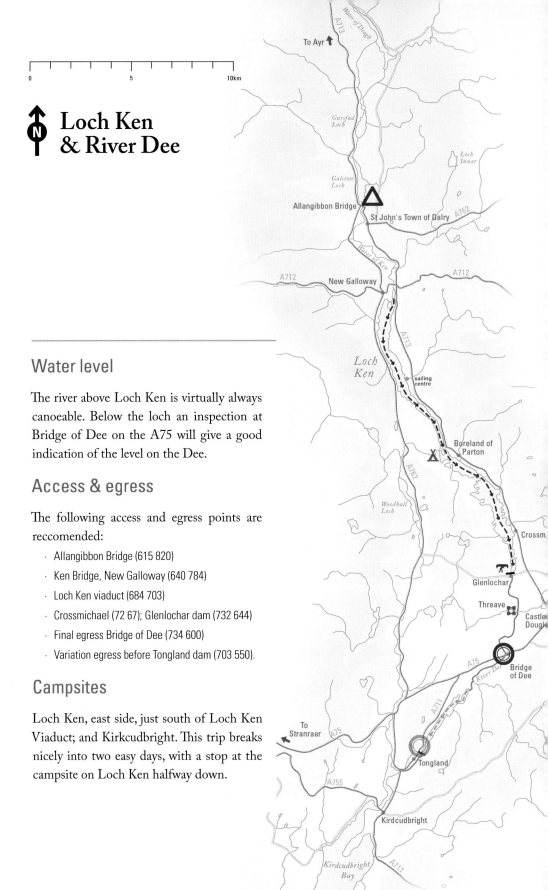

Loch Ken & River Dee

Water level

The river above Loch Ken is virtually always canoeable. Below the loch an inspection at Bridge of Dee on the A75 will give a good indication of the level on the Dee.

Access & egress

The following access and egress points are reccomended:

- · Allangibbon Bridge (615 820)
- · Ken Bridge, New Galloway (640 784)
- · Loch Ken viaduct (684 703)
- · Crossmichael (72 67); Glenlochar dam (732 644)
- · Final egress Bridge of Dee (734 600)
- · Variation egress before Tongland dam (703 550).

Campsites

Loch Ken, east side, just south of Loch Ken Viaduct; and Kirkcudbright. This trip breaks nicely into two easy days, with a stop at the campsite on Loch Ken halfway down.

Description

At Allangibbon Bridge near St John's Town of Dalry, the Water of Ken is a broad river with good water. Anglers are often found on this stretch. The quiet market town is to the left (east) of the river. The river is always paddleable below here and after 6km it passes under the Bridge of Ken, and imperceptibly becomes a loch with no current. New Galloway, another quiet little town, is 1km to the right.

The scenery changes from upland wooded hills to marsh and more open agricultural land. Kenmure Castle stands on the right bank.

Loch Ken is 17km long, and there is interest all the way down, with inlets and islands. Roads follow the loch down on both sides, the east side being easiest for access.

After 6km Loch Ken Sailing Centre is on the left bank, with canoes and dinghies for hire, instruction available, and a café. This upper part of the loch is ideal for canoe sailing. Small islands follow.

The Ken Viaduct (a disused railway line, now a footpath) provides a landmark at the narrowest part of the loch. There are power boats and water-skiing on this stretch. The campsite soon follows, with very easy access onto the water. The Black Water of Dee joins on the right. The loch then becomes interesting with islands, shallows and narrows. The scenery is more open, resembling a large marsh, and the way through islands is more difficult to see. The flats are crowded with wading birds. About halfway down this lower half of the loch there are narrows, followed by Crossmichael village on the left bank. At the end of Loch Ken is Glenlochar dam, with a lift over on the left side into the River Dee.

The Dee is a wide, deep river with few rapids. After a couple of kilometres Threave Island splits the river, with Threave Castle on the right-hand channel. There is a rapid where the two channels rejoin below the island. The large Lodge Island follows, with the main channel on the right then an old railway bridge and the main A75 Bridge of Dee. There is no easy access or egress here, nor vehicle parking. Castle Douglas is 4km to the left. Just downstream is the old Bridge of Dee, and a minor road on the left bank. Egress is possible (advised) on the right bank at this bridge. Parking is available in the village.

Variation

The remaining 6km has islands, shallows, and about halfway down this stretch becomes Tongland Loch. The egress is about 200m above the dam onto the busy A711 on the right bank. Park with care at a former lay-by, now fenced off. This egress is dangerous, due to the very small parking spot, and a very fast and busy main road. There is another possible exit point about 150m back upstream. Overall, if unsure, egress is better and safer at Bridge of Dee village.

Galloway Forest Park

The region immediately around the Ken and Dee is a large forest area planted for timber and used for a variety of outdoor activities.

There are walks, interpretive facilities, wildlife, guided events and a variety of accommodation, perhaps making this area the nearest to a North American national park.

A few miles north of the Ken and Dee route is Loch Doon, just over the border in Ayrshire, and a forest drive to Loch Bradan.

The Forest Park extends westwards as far as the A714 road from Newton Stewart to Girvan, and includes at its centre Glen Trool with a forest village and visitor centre. The route up Merrick, at 843m the highest hill in Southern Scotland, starts from Buchan at the end of the road. The area is worth visiting for the ancient oak woodland, at its best in autumn with a stunning array of colours from golden browns to russet reds. A scenic road runs from Glentrool village due north to Straiton in Ayrshire.

In the south of the area is Clatteringshaws Loch, on the A712 from Newton Stewart to New Galloway, with wild goats nearby.

The area offers children's activities, orienteering, mountain biking and much more. To find out full details and current events, go to Forestry Commission Scotland's website (www.scotland.forestry.gov.uk).

© Peebles on the River Tweed | VisitScotland/ScottishViewpoint

25 River Tweed

OS Sheets 72, 73, 74 & 75 | Peebles to Coldstream | 82km

Shuttle	50 miles, 1 hour 20 minutes, via A72, A6091, A699 and A698.
Portages	Some weirs might be portaged, depending on conditions. The 'caulds' are sloping weirs, most very easy and shallow-sloping. Makerstoun lower rapid (3–).
Start	△ Peebles (250 403).
Finish	◯ Coldstream caravan site (845 396)

Introduction

The Tweed is one of the original great Scottish touring rivers, a classic to be completed by canoeing visitors to Scotland, along with the Tay and Spey.

The Tweed valley has a fascinating history of land improvements and raids from over the border by the 'reivers'. It was always a rich area, as shown by the large farms and great houses still visible today. Many castles were built through the ages, and the remains and ruins are still there to be visited.

The upper valley is wooded and beautiful; the middle stretch through Galashiels and Melrose a bit more urban; from the A68 crossing down to Kelso is a broad agricultural valley; and Kelso

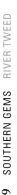

to Coldstream is different again, a busy angling river with high banks. There is interest all the way down, with frequent little towns, and the 'caulds' or weirs to wake you up. These are mostly of a very gradual gradient, sometimes no more than a gentle slope of small stones and easy to inspect or portage. The river gives a fulfilling trip of three or four days.

Water level

A look over most bridges in the middle section of the river will tell you what the level is like; a good place is at Fairnilee. The rapid and drops down river left should be easily negotiable, as well as the cauld above the bridge. Many paddlers feel that water levels have dropped in recent years, maybe due to agricultural abstraction.

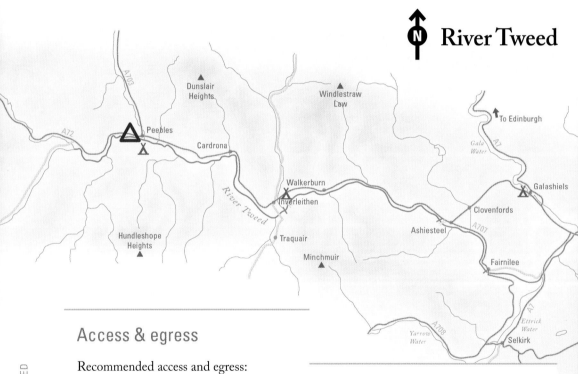

Access & egress

Recommended access and egress:

- Peebles bridge (250 403)
- Innerleithen campsite (340 366)
- Walkerburn bridge (361 369)
- Ashiesteel bridge (438 351)
- Fairnilee bridge (459 325)
- Old bridge off A7, with steps down (488 323)
- Melrose ford (544 345)
- Leaderfoot (575 346)
- Mertoun bridge (610 320)
- Kelso riverside, above the weir (723 343)
- A698 alongside river (80 39)
- Coldstream caravan site (845 396).

Campsites

There is a campsite at Peebles (although it is not on the river). Other possibilities are Inverleithen, Galashiels (4km away up the Gala Water, a good centre for touring the Borders), Melrose (off-river), and Lauder (10 miles to the north).

Rough camping is not possible or welcome down much of the valley. Avoid farmland and look for riverside woodland or islands.

© Springtime in the Tweed valley | VisitScotland/ScottishViewpoint

SUGGESTED ITINERARIES

A trip could be split thus: Peebles to Galashiels (32km), Galashiels to Kelso (30km) and Kelso to Coldstream (17km). Or alternatively: From Peebles to Inverleithen riverside campsite (14km), Inverleithen to Melrose (28km), then Melrose to Coldstream (45km).

Description

The Tweed rises in the extreme south-west corner of the Borders just over the hill from Moffat, at Tweed's Well, an obvious spring near the A701 Moffat to Edinburgh road. It can be canoed or kayaked in high water from only a few kilometres down the road as the valley bottom is quite flat. At Tweedsmuir road bridge there is a considerable fall. A traditional place for starting trips was Stobo, about 25km downstream. However, in most summers there is no chance of paddling loaded open canoes from here so distances are given from Peebles where the river has been joined by three small tributaries.

The start at Peebles is convenient and easy to find, a car park downstream of the bridge, on the right side of the river and only a short walk back over the bridge to the heart of this bustling town. The car park is large with toilets and easy access down onto the river. There are roads close to the river almost the whole way down.

This first day of some 32km is easy, pleasant paddling with occasional highlights. The 'new town' of Cardrona, 6km down, is marked by a hotel on the left bank and a housing estate on the right bank. Inverleithen follows after another 6km with a bridge, a rapid and the famous Traquair

© Mertoun Cauld, River Tweed | Eddie Palmer

House to the right. The village is a little way to the left, and after a disused railway bridge there is a convenient campsite on the left bank, one of the very few on the river.

Walkerburn has the first cauld on this stretch and the village, one of the Tweed valley wool settlements, is on the left bank. A long, pretty wooded stretch follows, a good bet for a secluded lunch stop. Ashiesteel rapid is upstream of an old bridge, with a settlement on the right bank. The line is down the right bank.

Up on the road on the left side is a roundabout where the main road leaves the river valley to take a shorter way over to Galashiels. A few kilometres on is the main excitement of this first day. It starts at Yair Cauld (often shallow) upstream of Fairnilee bridge and continues with Fairnilee rapid, a couple of drops on the left side of the river followed by fast water. Although not very difficult, Fairnilee can still give open canoe paddlers a shock. A useful parking spot below the bridge gives access for viewing the rapid.

The Ettrick Water joins from the right lower down, two road bridges follow and signs of civilisation announce the urban sprawl of Galashiels and Melrose, the population centre of the Borders. Abbotsford House (Sir Walter Scott's house) is on the right bank near the main road bridge. The egress is on the left bank, if completing a first day and going to the Galashiels campsite.

There is a good landing place for Melrose, 4km further on near the cauld which in this case is steep and rocky. This area is reached from the centre of Melrose by following signs for Newstead, and then taking a left turn for the Chain Bridge and riverside walk. This is a cul-de-sac with some parking. After a further 3km the river is spanned by the very obvious and high Leaderfoot Viaduct, a remnant of a picturesque borders railway line. The A68 bridge follows with access on the right bank. The Tweed winds between high wooded banks as it turns south for a time, and Scott's View and Monument are visible high up on the left bank for several miles. At Dryburgh Abbey on a long bend there is a hotel, the abbey, and a large house. Landing and parking are difficult here.

After the occasional island, rock ledge and shallows, the first excitement of this stretch is Mertoun Cauld, a weir just upstream of Mertoun bridge on the B6404. In high water, the extreme right may be the easiest route, in lowish water the centre is quite difficult. The scenery has changed to a much flatter agricultural landscape, hills and woods have mostly been left behind. A further 5km or so is a favourite amongst the caulds; Rutherford Cauld – just a bit larger than most, usually with a good flow and large waves. This cauld can just be seen from the A699.

Rutherford is the signal that the trickiest section of the Tweed is starting, especially for open canoes. Makerstoun House follows on the left bank, and then the three rapids traditionally known as Makerstoun rapids. In lowish water they all appear to be one long shallow stretch.

The first two rapids have channels down the right side. You will know that Lower Makerstoun rapid is approaching when the drop ahead appears substantial, and a row of cottages can be seen on the right bank (no vehicle access down from these cottages). Lower Makerstoun rapid presents little problem for kayaks but is tricky for open canoes, and warrants inspection. The usual route in medium water is down the extreme right side, over four drops, with the very narrow last one requiring some skill. In high to very high water there is a route down the left side of the river. The river now quietens down considerably and is shallow all the way down to Kelso, with the spectacular Floors Castle on the left bank.

As Kelso comes fully into view, the line of Kelso Cauld can be seen ahead. Above it there is a landing with car parking on the left bank. Kelso Cauld can be difficult and should be inspected. It is shot on the right in high water. The River Teviot joins from the right, then the old road bridge crosses the river, followed by another stony cauld and the new road bridge high above. There is a landing place on the right bank under the new road bridge, reached by a minor road.

The Tweed now widens and slows down. After 4km you reach Banff Mill weirs. It is wise to stop at the wall across the river and inspect, or if the river is high, land on left bank. The left-hand route has two steep and quite difficult drops, not recommended for open canoes. The best route is to start left, and immediately after the first drop, go sharply right, and turn left down the central chute. The rest of the way down is then simple.

Slow progress to Coldstream is enlivened by Carham Cauld (usually shootable), followed by a large island, and then the final event; a shallow cauld only 2km from the town. Coldstream appears on the left bank, and there is a good landing at an obvious green space which used to be a seasonal caravan site. You may have to park in the town, further back from the river. Coldstream is a pleasant border market town, with the A697 providing fast access either to England or back up to Edinburgh.

© Red Squirrel | Allan Bantick

Red squirrels

The Borders region of Scotland is home to red squirrels, as are the river valleys of the Spey and Dee with their extensive Scots pine woodlands. Most visitors from south of the border have never seen a red squirrel, and there is currently a battle royal taking place regarding 'what should be done about grey squirrels'.

The grey is quite a bit larger than the red, which is slight, with very obvious ear tufts. Greys have swiftly populated cities in Scotland. They are very common in Edinburgh and Glasgow and are now appearing in Dundee and Aberdeen. Although greys do not attack reds, they host a virulent pox to which the red is susceptible and have taken over their food supplies. The reds have retreated into conifer forests, particularly pine where they feed on cones with large seeds, as well as other seeds and acorns It is becoming clear that the culling of greys will not help the red, unless the appropriate habitat is kept. The practice of clear felling large areas of pine in one go has undoubtedly contributed to the demise of the red squirrel, and altering forestry practices will help them.

One certain sign of reds is a pile of munched pine cones under a tree – squirrels often seem to have a favourite tree to sit in and eat, often in pairs, as they are sociable animals. They are most often seen at dawn. If reds keep to the upper branches of trees they are safe, being predated on the ground by foxes, birds of prey or cars.

If camping on a river bank under pines, the sound of scampering animals and a 'chattering' at daybreak may well tell you that the red squirrel is present.

Scottish Outdoor Access Code

Access to the outdoors in Scotland is encouraged; visitors and locals have a right of responsible access. Scottish Natural Heritage is responsible for promoting and publicising the Scottish Outdoor Access Code (SOAC).

Where you have access rights to is not shown on Ordnance Survey maps, or any other map in Scotland. Respect people's privacy by staying away from houses and private gardens – access rights do not apply here.

Be discreet when either changing, or going to the toilet. If you are wild camping, choose a spot well away from roads and buildings, and be sure to remove all traces of your camp.

Access rights do not apply to motorised transport – do not use private (usually estate) roads without permission, and do not drive over rough country. Take care with parking, and do not block access or tracks or farm gates. You do, however, have a right, when not interfering with other people's livelihood or pleasure, to walk with a canoe from the road to the river or loch.

THE SCOTTISH OUTDOOR ACCESS CODE IS BASED ON THREE KEY PRINCIPLES AND THESE APPLY EQUALLY TO THE PUBLIC AND TO LAND MANAGERS.

RESPECT THE INTERESTS OF OTHER PEOPLE

Acting with courtesy, consideration and awareness is very important. If you are exercising access rights, make sure that you respect the privacy, safety and livelihoods of those living or working in the outdoors, and the needs of other people enjoying the outdoors. If you are a land manager, respect people's use of the outdoors and their need for a safe and enjoyable visit.

CARE FOR THE ENVIRONMENT

If you are exercising access rights, look after the places you visit and enjoy, and leave the land as you find it. If you are a land manager, help maintain the natural and cultural features which make the outdoors attractive to visit and enjoy.

TAKE RESPONSIBILITY FOR YOUR OWN ACTIONS

If you are exercising access rights, remember that the outdoors cannot be made risk-free and act with care at all times for your own safety and that of others. If you are a land manager, act with care at all times for people's safety.

Getting more advice and information

The Scottish Outdoor Access Code cannot cover every possible situation, setting or activity. Free information and advice on access rights and responsibilities, and on who to contact in your local authority, is available online at:

www.outdooraccess-scotland.com

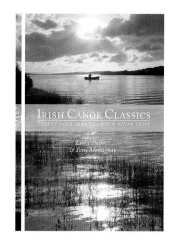
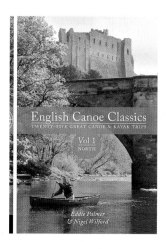
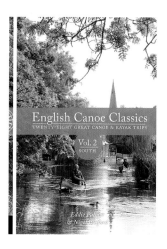